Blogging FOR
BLISS

Blogging
FOR BLISS

Crafting Your Own Online Journal

A GUIDE FOR CRAFTERS,
ARTISTS & CREATIVES OF ALL KINDS

Tara Frey

LARK BOOKS

A Division of Sterling Publishing Co., Inc.
New York / London

**Red Lips 4 Courage
Communications, Inc.**
www.redlips4courage.com

Eileen Cannon Paulin
President

Catherine Risling
Director of Editorial

Erika Kotite
Development Director

Editor: Rebecca Ittner

Art Director: Jocelyn Foye

Copy Editors: Mary Beth P. Adomaitis,
Catherine Risling, Ashlea Scaglione

Library of Congress
Cataloging-in-Publication Data

Frey, Tara.
  Blogging for bliss : crafting your own
online journal / Tara Frey. -- 1st ed.
     p. cm.
  Includes index.
  ISBN 978-1-60059-511-0
(pb-pbk. : alk. paper)
  1. Blogs--Design. I. Title.
  TK5105.8884.F74 2009
  006.7--dc22
                           2009003807

10 9 8 7 6 5 4 3 2 1

First Edition

Published by Lark Books,
A Division of Sterling Publishing Co., Inc.
New York / London

Text © 2009, Tara Frey
Photography © 2009, Red Lips 4 Cour-
age Communications, Inc.
Illustrations © 2009, Red Lips 4 Courage
Communications, Inc.

Distributed in Canada by Sterling
Publishing, c/o Canadian Manda Group,
165 Dufferin Street, Toronto, Ontario,
Canada M6K 3H6

Distributed in the United Kingdom by
GMC Distribution Services, Castle Place,
166 High Street, Lewes, East Sussex,
England BN7 1XU

Distributed in Australia by Capricorn Link
(Australia) Pty Ltd., P.O. Box 704, Wind-
sor, NSW 2756 Australia

If you have questions or comments
about this book, please contact:
Lark Books
67 Broadway
Asheville, NC 28801
(828) 253-0467

Manufactured in China

ISBN 13: 978-1-60059-511-0

For information about custom editions,
special sales, premium and corporate
purchases, please contact Sterling Special
Sales Department at (800) 805-5489 or
specialsales@sterlingpub.com.

For Dad. The best storyteller I know.

Welcome

Daisy Cottage
My 1922 Dream Come True

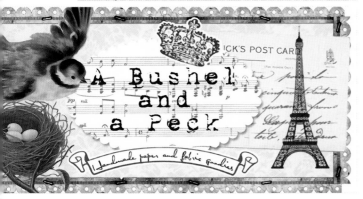

A Bushel
and
a Peck

decor8
fresh finds for hip spaces

weekly: *blog* That Unreliable Girl   *book* Easy Elegance

"As a writer and interior design consultant, I created decor8 to catalog beautiful finds and to inspire others." -Holly Becker

Bari J.™
A journal of creative inspiration.

Contents

> In Chapter 1 you will meet …
> *Elsa Mora • Kim McCole • Amanda Soule • Alicia Paulson •*
> *Jenny Heid • Jeanne Griffin • Betz White • Pam Vieira-McGinnis*

> In Chapter 2 you will meet …
> *Tracy Porter • Serena Thompson & Teri Edwards • Chris Glynn •*
> *Alys Geertsen • Corey Amaro • Janet Coon • Monica Solorio-Snow •*
> *Happy Harris*

Finding My Bliss

There are blogs and blog communities for every subject imaginable. In this book we feature the creative ones—art blogs, craft blogs, quilting blogs, sewing blogs, vintage ephemera blogs, and more—that help you get lost for a while, and leave you feeling inspired, renewed, and refreshed.

On the following pages I will take you on a creative journey. From blank screens to beautiful, colorful pages, you'll be inspired to share your talents and awaken the creative spirit that lies within. Whether it's all new to you, or you have a blog and are looking to update it, this book will introduce you to the blissful blogs out there and tell you what you need to know to hold court with some of the most amazingly creative and inspirational bloggers of our time. You'll find your voice, and learn how to connect with others around the globe.

Creative blogs are the personal journals of the 21st century. Instead of holding tightly guarded secrets, these online journals are open for all to see and read. For a growing number of creative souls, both amateur and professional, blogging is an immensely satisfying means of artistic expression. Done for pure pleasure and inspiration, creative blogging is not only an avenue to share yourself and your interests, it's also a wonderful way to find like-minded individuals.

I began my online journal in 2004. Journaling has always been important to me and I find that jotting down thoughts onto paper is a therapeutic and natural experience. I started keeping a journal as a child and took creative writing classes in college as an artistic release. For me, blogging was simply the next step in my creative journey. I came to blogging as a result of an online business venture. In 2001, I began selling vintage finds on eBay, and then opened my own virtual home décor boutique, Bella Pink, in 2004. When my little shop received national attention in magazines, I began to get a flood of emails with questions and comments.

This got me thinking about finding a way to communicate directly with those who visited my site, getting to know them, and letting them get to know me. The answer was to start a blog. My goal was to create a place where I could share my thoughts and ramblings, and readers could leave comments, just as though we were chatting at the cash register of a real brick-and-mortar store.

Writing my first post, I never imagined that my little blog, now called "tara frey: {typing out loud}" where I blather on about nothing and sometimes something, would connect with so many people and receive the attention it has over the years. People really read it! They left comments with their own blog links, so I did some peeking around of my own. What I discovered was an incredibly expansive creative blogging community that connects people from all over the world. Wandering among fabric mavens, digital scrappers, mixed-media artists, crafters, designers, and antique junkers, I was Alice in Wonderland who never, ever wanted to find her way back home.

As I meandered along, reading various posts, blogs with great images were the ones that most attracted me. I wanted my blog to give readers some-

thing I enjoyed seeing: large, crisp, and inspiring imagery. I decided to trade in my point-and-shoot for a big daddy digital SLR camera that makes picture taking a more rewarding experience. Unlike their smaller counterpart, the easy-to-use point-and-shoot camera, digital SLR cameras, or DSLRs, provide an accurate preview of framing right before a picture is taken, and lets users choose from a variety of interchangeable lenses. Many DSLRs provide an accurate preview of depth of field.

With this new toy I snapped all types of photos. Treasures found at flea markets, catching my kids doing something adorable, a day out shopping, or the perfect flower in our garden; all were fair game for my blossoming blog. Once the photo was placed on my blog, the words came easily.

So do some research, figure out what inspires you, and get started. If you build it, they will come. If you blog, they will read. So let's start blogging!

tara frey

TARA'S FAVORITE POSTS

- *12 years...*
- *A Written Note...*
- *Come Window Shop With Me...*
- *I do...*
- *Imagination...*
- *Pick Your Own...*
- *The Color Purple...*

TARA'S CORNER BOOKSTORE

The French-Inspired Home
By Kaari Meng, French General

Apples for Jam: A Colorful Cookbook
By Tessa Kiros

Falling Cloudberries: A World of Family Recipes
By Tessa Kiros

Crowns & Tiaras: Add a Little Sparkle, Glitter & Glamour to Every Day
By Kerri Judd & Danyel Montecinos

Chapter 1
WHY BLOG FOR BLISS

It's in our human nature to want to connect with other people, to explore and to be inspired. Blogging for bliss means many things to many bloggers, but in the end it's all about connecting, learning, and giving back by inspiring others. With just a few clicks of a mouse you can be transported into a creative and inspiring community where quilters can learn new techniques, moms can connect with other moms, and artists can share their creations and gain recognition. Creative blogs are wonderful and welcoming places, introducing countless avenues to express one's passions.

Websites like Facebook and MySpace, and blogs like those found on TypePad, Blogger/Blogspot, and WordPress, are all forms of social networking. Social networking is not just the way of the future; it is right now, in the present.

When I bought tickets to my 20th high school reunion, I emailed the organizer to ask if she knew who was going to attend. She told me to join Facebook, to enter our high school name and the year we graduated, and to set up a profile. This is the new social order. Within 20 minutes I was re-connecting with old friends, laughing over old times, looking at their children's photos, and reading about their careers and families. How exciting! Though different than blogging, I loved being able to have online conversations with friends.

Blissful bloggers will excitedly tell you about the friends they have all over the world, all "united under one blogosphere." Blogging allows us to meet and reach people from all walks of life, all races and nationalities, and different political and religious viewpoints. Blissful blogging connects us by one common thread: creativity.

Instead of curling up with a magazine and a cup of tea, many people escape into their favorite blogs where they can find comfort, humor, answers, recipes, and inspiration. But blogging is much more than reading or writing; it is conversation. The conversation begins with your post and continues as readers write comments on your blog or talk about your posts on their own blogs. Where else but on a blog can you comment directly to a favorite fabric designer and tell her about the new book tote you just made using her fabrics; or to a magazine editor whose story you just finished reading and loved so much that it went into an inspiration binder for design ideas; or to a creative mama, who inspired you to turn off the television, get out the glue and construction paper, and do a craft project with the kids? This instant-gratification element of blogging is fun, empowering, and uniquely satisfying.

Daisy Cottage is a blog written by Kim McCole about cottage life in Florida.

Lisa Tutman Oglesby is a talented crafter who gives tutorials on every craft project imaginable on her blog.

willows95988.typepad.com

French Christmas Tradition no. 2

A papillote is a chocolate (or candied fruit) that is wrapped in tissue paper with a note written on it. The sparkly golden exterior paper has fringed ends. Some

Tongue in Cheek is a beautiful and inspiring blog about American Corey Amaro's life in France.

stitchindye.blogspot.com

dd to that the fact that there is no basting involved. No mc urniture so that I can attempt to smoothly layout the backi atting and then spend the next three hours scooting aroun

Business is the focal point of Malka Dubrawsky's blog, A Stitch in Dye. Beautiful images of her fabric and quilts help Malka keep her customers informed.

Screen Gems

There are countless beautiful creative blogs written by blissful bloggers from all walks of life. Some bloggers hail from the countryside and write about their homes and families, and may also share decorating ideas and recipes right alongside stories about the day's activities. Others call the city their home and blog about their business, making sure to include stories about their customers and information about new products, as well as thoughts about urban life. Sharing handmade goods is at the heart of many creative blogs. Many of these bloggers include how-to projects and ideas for finding inspiration.

Bliss vs. Business

Creative forces—from altered artists, fabric mavens, and quilting divas, to jewelry artisans, photographers, and interior designers—have established blogs on the Internet. Some blog for bliss, some blog for business, and some have meshed the two seamlessly together.

For those who blog for bliss, it's a need for personal expression and a passion for sharing their lives or crafts that drives their blogs. Although they receive no monetary gain, these bloggers will tell you that the satisfaction of giving, sharing, and inspiring others is priceless.

On the business side, blogs are designed to help promote creative wares or services, and if done well, they can be an invaluable business tool. Those who blog for business live creatively; their businesses, personal lives, and friendships are all approached through their creative spirit and it shows in their blogs. Whether they promote products and services through sidebar links or talk about business in every post, their blogs are beautiful and inspiring.

The creation of community and new friendships is a benefit for every blogger, no matter their motivation. Knowing there are creative people out there in blogdom who will listen and support you is a wonderful thing.

Set the Tone

There are several factors to consider when finding your voice in the creative blogging world. Taking the time to think about these points before writing your first post will send you in the right direction. Some things to consider:

What is your purpose?

Are you a mother who crafts and/or an artist who paints? Being a successful creative blogger doesn't take a lot of work, but you do need to know who you are. You don't have to be crafty to host a creative, inspiring blog. Your words and photos can be your craft. My blog is about my life, little bits and pieces shared in posts. I knit on occasion and I'm a flea market junkie. I find that most responses and feedback comes when I talk about my family, my home, and my latest discovery at the flea market.

Who is your audience?

Though creative blogs are by definition a blend of subjects, deciding who you want to reach is key to crafting a successful blog. Think about your passions: Are you a 20-something crafter who lives an eco-conscious life or a busy mom and entrepreneur who loves all things vintage? Deciding on an audience will make designing and writing your blog much easier.

Keep in mind that creative blog readers come to your journal to escape, so it can be disappointing or uncomfortable for them when they see political rants, religious overtones, or foul language. If you want that type of blog, you may be in the wrong neighborhood.

What do you want to say?

If you speak *your* truth, you'll discover that words come more easily. Pretending life is perfect is not realistic. Readers connect more when you talk about things the way they *really* are—like how you stayed in your jammies all day sewing in your studio, and before you knew it the clock read 3 p.m.!

On her blog, Inside A Black Apple, Emily Martin blends life, art, and business in her posts.

Heather Bullard weaves together business, artist events, show information, and how-to tips on her blog, Vintage Inspired Living.

When I changed the name of my blog, I wrote about it in the post that day. Readers were very supportive in their comments.

Artist Sandra Evertson chose her name for the title of her blog. This is a great choice for creative bloggers who also have art or crafts to sell.

The Name Game

Choosing a name for your blog can be compared to naming your first-born. Your online journal is an important part of your creative world and a personal journey. Naming it might seem like an easy task; however, it's important to choose a name wisely because it might turn out to be a forever thing.

Once you choose your blog name and are given a URL for your blog (that's what people type in the address bar of their browser in order to find you), you can't just simply change your mind and change your blog's URL. This is a technical issue and a practical issue. Blog hosts don't allow bloggers to just change their URL and keep everything associated with the original blog address. Changing URLs is like moving to a new house—you have to bring everything with you and set it all up again. People will know you by your chosen blog name and address—changing it can make it confusing for your readers to find you. You will want your blog name to be one you can live with for a long time.

Many creative bloggers use their own name. The upside to using your name? It's easy for blog readers to remember. The downside? Loss of all anonymity. If you prefer to keep your identity under wraps, then of course this is not the choice for you.

Before you decide on a blog name, ask a few trusted friends what they think. It's easy to get tunnel vision when trying to come up with a name; a fresh perspective can help you understand how the name can be interpreted by others.

Some things to consider when naming your blog
- What do you want your creative blog to say about you?
- What is it going to be about? Your life? Your crafts? Or both?
- Keep it simple. Be careful not to choose a name that is hard to remember, too long, or has dashes or underscores, for example: this_blogname-is_super_cali_fragilistically_long.com.

Changing Identities

Regrets, I have a few…When naming my blog, I chose the name of my online store at the time, Bella Pink. I wasn't thinking ahead. Yes, pink will always be "bella" or "beautiful," but will it be *me* forever?

Eventually, other exciting opportunities arrived and I couldn't keep up the store, so I closed its Web doors. I wanted to continue my blog but found myself stuck with the name. I thought if I changed it, all of the link-backs would be lost. (Linkbacks are links to my blog from blogs that have referenced or linked to my blog over the years.) I also thought I would have to transfer the three to four years of posts I had made on my old blog. It all seemed so daunting. I had to come up with an easier solution.

The answer? Domain mapping. This is a simple process of purchasing a domain name in your new blog name, then pointing it to your blog URL. Every blog host has tutorials on how to do this. I decided to rename my blog Tara Frey—it's me and it's simple.

I purchased the domain name, tarafrey.com, and then directed it to land on my blog at www.bellapink.typepad.com. Many of the blogs I read daily, including some of those in this book, don't match their URL address, so if you decide to change your name down the road, you won't be alone.

Take a Break

Blogging for bliss should be cathartic, therapeutic, and most of all, fun. Once it becomes a "chore," most bloggers will tell you that is when it's time to take a blog break. There may be times when life just gets too hectic for you to blog—projects are due, a loved one is ill, or the house is under construction.

Hang up the "taking a break" sign and let your readers know you'll be back. They'll understand and look forward to your return. Blogging should always feel like an option and never an obligation.

To notify readers of her upcoming vacation, Bari J. Ackerman posted this pretty graphic.

Elsa Mora took a blogiday to spend some much-needed time taking care of family business, and talked about it in this post.

Find her: elsita.typepad.com

Blogs about: crafting, paper cutting, personal life

Elsa Mora treasures the human connection, the feedback, and the amazing energy that comes from every single person who decides to leave a comment on her blog. A creative spirit with a penchant for paper cutting, Elsa was born in Cuba, graduated from art school, and became an art teacher for a few years. After that, she worked in an art gallery, then decided to chuck it all and become a full-time artist. She moved to Los Angeles in 2001.

When she began her blog, Elsa honestly didn't know what it was going to be about. She only knew that it would be a virtual space where she could create her own planet. "The sheer thought of that was exciting to me," Elsa recalls. She saw this as a new adventure and believes the magic of any new adventure is being open to whatever happens in the process.

Elsa's blog is herself in words and pictures. What you see is what she is. Her blog is about her life and all the things she cares about, one post at a time. Her entries are inspired by anything that makes her think, whatever her passion is at the moment. Elsa says her blog has changed her life in a great way, as she considers connecting with others one of the most important things that motivates people.

Elsa advises anyone thinking of starting a blog to not be intimidated. Start it as a way of dedicating some time to yourself, to keep your mind active and your senses awake. Elsa is convinced that keeping a blog makes you more aware of everything around you and it's a wonderful tool to learn more about yourself. She advises to not think of your blog as an Internet competition. Keep it real, be yourself, and write about the things you care about. Enjoy it, and the rest will fall into place.

Elsa's favorite daily reads: resurrectionfern.typepad.com, thecarrotbox.com, williamhorberg.typepad.com

Find her: deardaisycottage.typepad.com
Blogs about: daily life, her dog Maggie, home décor, shopping

Enter the "1922 dream cottage" of Kim McCole, whose wildly popular blog, Daisy Cottage, has become the favorite of countless creative bloggers since she started it in 2006. Kim is truly a blissful blogger; she has no boutique or crafts to sell. Instead, her craft is to "write and inspire."

Kim offers a glimpse into her life at her sweet and sunny Florida home. The blog is chock-full of beautiful photos, simple inspirations, and her blogstar dog, Maggie. Her entries are inspired by the simple pouring of a bowl of cereal and the perfect look of the morning light. This prompts her to grab her camera and capture the loveliness that is her world at Daisy Cottage. Kim also loves to share anything silly or cute that her dog does,

family moments, or even a trip to a local store that she thinks her readers would enjoy.

When asked why she thinks her blog has become so popular without any boutique or items to sell, Kim says she receives countless emails from readers who consider her blog an escape from their stress. "With the click of a button, they can 'sit' on the front porch at Daisy Cottage and visit for a while," she explains.

Kim takes her readers with her wherever she goes—on vacation or on antiquing adventures—that is the most blissful advantage of blogging.

Kim's favorite daily reads: backporchmusings. blogspot.com, southernhospitality-rhoda.blogspot.com, theoldpaintedcottage.blogspot.com

THANK YOU!

Flea Extravaganza!

BLOG CANDY
Click On "Blog Candy" To See My Blogroll! Lovely Places For You To Visit!

Find her: soulemama.typepad.com

Blogs about: baking, family, gardening, knitting, sewing

Amanda Soule, from Portland, Maine, has become a "mama" blogging phenomenon. A two-time author and mother of four, Amanda has built up a wide audience that likes nothing better than to peek in daily for a nourishing dose of knitting, sewing, embroidery, baking, and gardening.

This didn't happen overnight, though. Amanda started her blog on a whim in 2005 as a way to keep in touch with faraway friends and family. "I found it was a great way to document the sometimes mundane moments of parenting little ones," Amanda says. In retrospect, Amanda thinks she was really looking for a reason to write every day—an art she has always loved but didn't do regularly.

Photography and writing are important elements to Amanda's blog. She is first to admit that she is not an expert in any of these creative endeavors, but she enjoys them all nonetheless. Amanda loves the daily rhythm of writing and photography and believes it helps her to slow down and reflect and focus on the joys, beauty, and little moments that matter most to her.

For Amanda, the biggest challenge in blogging has been the negative comments. "I suppose it's only natural that as readership of a blog grows, so, too, does the criticism and negative feedback," Amanda says. "It's been a challenge and an important lesson." Her solution? To be authentic in living her life, in her writing, and in what she believes is important.

Amanda offers ad space to sponsors on her blog, a decision she made after long and careful consideration. She is grateful for the opportunity to make a small income from her blog, while at the same time, matching up readers/customers with crafters/businesses who share similar styles, aesthetics, and values. "I feel sort of like a matchmaker, which is fun," she says.

Amanda posts five to six days a week and sometimes needs a blog break. She feels that the timeouts are a wonderful way to recharge, reflect on blogging, and keep things fresh. She sometimes switches to a "photo-only" project for a bit or she'll often call in her most popular guest blogger, "Soule Papa," her husband.

Find her: rosylittlethings.typepad.com
Blogs about: baking, business, crafting, daily life, her dog Clover Meadow

Alicia Paulson, a multi-talented crafter from Portland, Oregon, describes her blog as a love letter to her husband. In it, she records the prosaic details of the daily life they feel very privileged to have together. "It is a collection of crafts, pets, travels, breakfasts, baking, dinners, shop talk, and life talk," Alicia says. "Mostly, it's me rambling to myself."

These ramblings have made her one of the most widely read bloggers in the blogosphere. "I'm still flabbergasted that people read it," she says with real humility.

Alicia began her blog in 2005 as a place where she could stop, relax, and appreciate her life. She started the blog at a time of intense stress. She didn't place any expectations on herself when it came to her postings (and still doesn't).

Alicia wants her blog to continue to be a place where she can be herself, discovering new things about herself in the process of writing and sharing what she thinks and learning from the things that people share with her.

Alicia says that blogging has brought a new audience to her work, but she never blogs because she thinks it will help her business. She does it because it has helped her life and that's what she really cares about.

Her entries are inspired by what's going on around the house. Sometimes the posts are very practical and literal; sometimes she has been thinking about something and needs a place to work out her thoughts. The superstar on her blog is Clover Meadow, her Corgi dog. She doubts anyone would read the blog if they didn't get a glimpse of the famous Miss Clover.

Alicia's advice for new bloggers: "Just do it, baby!" She's not one who thinks you should know exactly what your blog should be or say. "Let it grow and change organically," she advises. "Let it be a little time of reflection and sharing in your life. Just do it, every day, and see what happens."

Alicia's favorite daily reads: loobylu.com, yarnstorm. blogs.com, yvestown.com

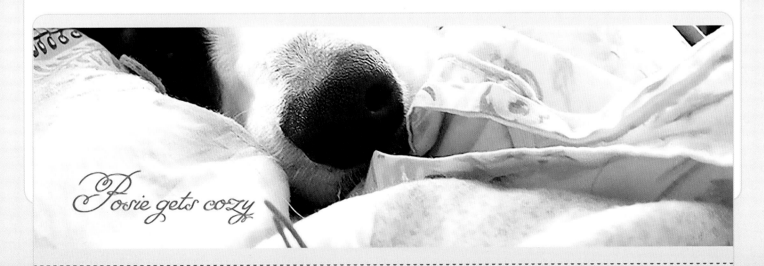

Posie gets cozy

JENNY HEID: Everyday is a Holiday

Find her: everyday-is-a-holiday.blogspot.com
Blogs about: art, collectibles, décor

Jenny Heid's blog actually takes its name from the business she shares with her husband, Aaron. Jenny and Aaron have been in business together as artists since they were teens, creating everything from murals to their own line of hand-painted furniture.

A few years ago Aaron was in a near-fatal car accident and his recovery was long and arduous. This experience brought a brand new outlook on life for the two artists. The name Everyday is a Holiday was their new way of life, and it is extremely important to Jenny. "After being so close to tragedy we started to see every new day as a gift," she explains.

Their artwork soon changed to fit the moniker and they focused on works that captured life's celebrations—holiday art, birthday cakes, fun vintage collectibles, and party decorations. When Jenny first started her blog, this was the only name she considered because her art and blog share an identical vision.

Jenny began her blog in 2006 and always thought of it as a lifeline to the outside world. As an artist working from home, she spends nearly all her time locked away inside. Jenny wanted an outlet to share her new creations, flea market finds, and decorating ideas. She knew that the give and take with other bloggers would be beneficial to her creatively. "There's nothing quite like getting to bounce my ideas off of hundreds of other like-minded people without having to leave my studio," Jenny says.

Jenny advises that in order to write a blog you have to read a lot of blogs. Find those kindred spirits who will become your readers. If you fall in love with a blog, Jenny says, you must leave comments and link it to your blog. Then sit back and watch how fast word spreads.

Jenny's favorite daily reads: artsymama.blogspot.com, rosylittlethings.typepad.com, theblackapple.typepad.com

JEANNE GRIFFIN: A Bushel and a Peck

Find her: bushelandapeck.typepad.com

Blogs about: accessories, clothing, her children, mixed-media art

Jeanne Griffin, a wife and mom of three, named her blog after a beautiful lullaby her mother used to sing to her when she was young. A Bushel and a Peck, her blog since the summer of 2008, is a place for her to share her creations and promote her Etsy business in a casual way. However, she finds that her most natural blog posts are inspired by her role as a mother and all the heartwarming stories that come along with it.

This WAHM (work-at-home-mom) is a mixed-media artist who also designs clothing for children as well as vintage-inspired items for women. She is thrilled when she sees her creations used on her customers' blogs. "How many designers ever get to see what happens to the items they put so much effort into creating after they leave the shop?" Jeanne says. She considers it an exciting way to connect to her customer base, which is growing rapidly.

Just like so many of her customers and blog readers, Jeanne is devoted to her family but she also has a deep desire to create and explore her artistic sensibilities—in short, she is trying to find the right balance in her life. Jeanne puts it into perspective by saying, "We love being mothers, wives, friends, and sisters, but we also want something that is just ours."

When asked what her blog has taught her about herself, Jeanne candidly admits, "It taught me that I'm not as horrible of a writer as I thought I was. I'm not perfect, but I have really enjoyed writing again. It used to come so easily and hopefully it will get better and better the more I do it."

Jeanne's favorite daily reads: blissfulliving-domesticbliss.blogspot.com, mcmasterandstorm.blogspot.com, nieniedialogues.blogspot.com

BETZ WHITE: Betz White

Find her: blog.betzwhite.com
Blogs about: children, family, projects, tutorials

In the spring of 2006, Betz White left her corporate apparel design job to freelance from home and spend time with her kids. An incredibly talented designer, Betz now creates whimsical felted wool products from home. A website went up first to give her a place to show and sell her wares, then she started her blog. "My husband is a Web designer and created betzwhite.com after I started selling my work at art fairs and on consignment websites," says Betz. "As a designer, I knew I wanted to use my own name for my website and blog because I wanted my work to be synonymous with me. I also wanted the name of my business to be something far-reaching and not too limiting, trendy, or sounding dated in years to come."

Betz started blogging as a means to share and talk about her work. "When I left my corporate job, I went through an adjustment period," she says. "I felt very isolated and missed the feedback one gets when working with other designers. The blog allowed me to find kindred spirits within the online crafting community, which provided a little show-and-tell as well as inspiration from following the creative blogs of others."

Having a blog has given Betz opportunities she could never have expected. She is now an accomplished author and has appeared on "The Martha Stewart Show." She recalls, "Originally the blog helped to give my work some visibility. That's how the producers for Martha Stewart's show found me."

But, fame and fortune are not what she loves most about blogging. "It's given me a voice in the crafting community and has shown me that I enjoy sharing my knowledge of my craft," says Betz, who is also a talented photographer. "I find the crafting community to be very supportive and positive and as a result I have made friends with people all over the country and the world."

To anyone starting a blog, Betz offers the following advice: "Offer them information, entertainment, inspiration, or whatever will give them a reason to come back and visit again. I believe balancing those things creates a blog that is appealing for you to maintain and for readers to frequent."

Betz' favorite daily reads: blog.craftzine.com, rosylittlethings.typepad.com, annamariahorner.blogspot.com, blairpeter.typepad.com, susanbanderson.blogspot.com

betz white
felted wool artfully stitched

About Me

PAM VIEIRA-McGINNIS: PamKittyMorning

Find her: pamkittymorning.blogspot.com
Blogs about: family, humor, life, quilting, sewing

Pam Vieira-McGinnis describes her blog as being a joke "in the sense that it's about nothing, kind of like Seinfeld." Her readers, though, find her sense of humor and her ability to find joy in the little things refreshing and addictive. She says, "I think the offbeat posts get the most response, my willingness to laugh at myself." When asked what makes her blog unique, Pam replies, "I think mostly my flair for the ridiculous."

Once she found the world of blogging, it didn't take Pam long to start one of her own. "I started blogging on a whim, a girlfriend kept urging me to do it," she says. "I had just discovered blogging a month before. I didn't know if I'd have anything to say."

Even the name of her blog came about as a result of Pam's blog surfing. "Every morning I was reading blogs and drinking my coffee," she says. "Then I found kitty-craft.com, a Japanese craft product blog. I was crazy about it. As I was reading the blog, a friend asked what I was doing. I said, 'Having a Pam Kitty Morning.' The name just stuck, and I still love it."

Pam suggests doing a search on your desired blog name before making it yours. "Google your intended blog name; you don't want to get confused with something or someone else," she advises.

For anyone thinking about starting a blog, Pam shares this advice: Decide what you will and will not blog about before you post. "Coming up with ideas for posts can be challenging at first," says Pam. "Keep a list of things you'd like to talk about so you have something to fall back on. Also, consider your family members and your kids. Once you put it out there, you don't know who will read it. Or what they'll say."

A natural curiosity about life makes blogging especially enjoyable for Pam. "Since I was a kid, I've always wondered how other people go about their days, what they do, what they think," she says. "Blogs are like a walk through the neighborhood, really. I'm so inspired by the things other people do. I'm also interested in what other people think about. I think one of the great things is seeing how other people live."

Blogging has done much more than satisfy her curiosity, though. Pam says, "I could never have imagined all the wonderful opportunities blogging has brought my way, or how many wonderful friendships I've made. I've been very lucky that way."

Pam's favorite daily reads: the-latebloomer.blogspot.com, sandyberry.typepad.com, fredashive.blogspot.com, thehappyzombie.com

she wished every morning was a ...
PAMKITTYMORNING

Chapter 2 TOOLS OF THE TRADE

Online journals date back to 1994. Freelance journalist Justin Hall is widely recognized as one of the earliest bloggers. He began his online journal, Justin's Links from the Underground, while a student at Swathmore College in Pennsylvania—five years before the term "blog" was in existence. In the next few years the blog community grew slowly and was made up of folks who knew their way around a keyboard and had a good grasp on technology.

In 1997, writer Jorn Barger coined the term "weblog" to describe his process of writing about the Web as he surfed the Internet. Peter Merholz, another early adopter

of online journals, shortened the term to "wee-blog" on his blog in 1999. He wrote about it in a May 2002 post (peterme.com): "Sometime in April or May of 1999 (I can't say for sure when I exactly did it), I posted in the sidebar of my home page: 'For What It's Worth: I've decided to pronounce the word weblog as wee- blog. Or blog for short.'" Peter says, "I didn't think much of it. I was just being silly, shifting the syllabic break one letter to the left. I started using the word in my posts, and some folks, when emailing me, would use it, too." His "silliness" was the creation of the word that would forever describe the phenomenon of blogging.

Pyra Labs, now owned by Google, launched Blogger/Blogspot, its Web-based and easy-to-use blog-building software. Merholz said of its launch: "Blog would have likely died a forgotten death had it not been for one thing: In August of 1999, Pyra Labs released Blogger. And with that, the use of "blog" grew with the tool's success." With Blogger, suddenly you didn't have to be tech savvy to have a blog. This is when blogging really took off. (Other blog services including Pitas and Groksoup launched around the same time, but didn't catch on like Blogger.)

From these early days up to the present, blogging has grown to reach all aspects of society—from technology, education, politics, and religion to music, crafting, fashion, and alternative lifestyles—and is now part of our social make-up. According to Technorati, an Internet search engine that indexes and searches blogs, there are an estimated 112.8 million online blogs worldwide, though not all of them are active blogs.

So what makes a blog different than a traditional website? A blog is a type of website supported by a content management system that provides a collection of features including a home page where the latest content automatically appears on top and earlier posts appear in backwards order (most recent on top), comments, categories, tags, blogrolls, and more. Blogs allow users to do much more than just write and share

Jenny Harris writes about some of her new offerings in a post from May 2008. Dated entries are just one of the ways in which blogs differ from traditional websites.

Jenny Harris received dozens of comments in response to a post in her blog, All Sorts, about her cute clothespin dolls. Comments are a unique feature to blogs.

Holly Becker self-hosts her blog, Decor8, using word press.org. Doing so has allowed her the freedom to build a blog uniquely suited to her audience.

Claire Robinson has owned her self-hosted blog, Loobylu, for more than a decade. Over the years, she has changed the look and feel of her blog as needed.

text. You can include photos and photo galleries, audio and video clips, podcasts, widgets, and other interactive tools, and have separate pages for content like your profile. Historically, websites have been more static, with visitors just able to read content and purchase goods and services, but not truly interact or converse with anyone behind the scenes.

As the Web continues to grow and change, many traditional websites are being built with links to blogs or built with blogging tools so that visitors can receive information in a traditional static format as well as experience blog benefits like comments and dated entries.

Deciding What You Want

The first decision you will make in your journey to creating a blog is what type of blog software platform to use. But in order to choose what will work best for you, you will need to have a good idea of how you want your blog to look and what you want to do on your blog. Take notice of the blogs that you frequent and look at what blog software they use. Jot down what appeals to you (for example, text presented in a two-column or three-column style, banner appearance, sidebars, etc.); make notes of your likes and dislikes.

Another thing to consider is your level of technical skill. Are you a tech-savvy creative soul and know your way around programs and coding languages like HTML? Or are you a Web newbie or don't want to worry about all that technical stuff? If you are facing a big learning curve, you will need to factor in extra time for research and study. This may also impact your choice of blog platform. Once you take the design and technological issues under consideration, choose the blog software platform that meets your needs. We will discuss subjects like blog set-up and posting in Chapter 3, but for now here are some basics. There are two main types of blog software platforms available: self-hosted and domain-hosted.

Self-hosted platforms

These software packages are installed by blog authors to run on their own servers. Because this choice of platform requires more knowledge about navigating around the Web and using HTML coding, it may not be the best choice for those new to blogging.

Advantages of self-hosted blog platforms

- Full control: You can build your blog just the way you want it.
- Add-ons and plug-ins: Increase the abilities of the blog platform.
- Truly unique URL: It's more professional, supports branding efforts, and is easy to remember.

Disadvantages of self-hosted blog platforms

- Difficult set-up: Self-hosted blogging platforms have a complicated set-up process.
- Does not automatically update: You must install updates yourself.
- Additional costs: Though some of the software platforms are free to use (i.e. wordpress.org, Drupal), by the time you figure in the cost of buying a domain name, signing up with a host provider, and designing the blog, your blog is not free.

Developer-hosted software platforms

This is the most popular type of software used by creative bloggers. With developer-hosted software platforms, they do the work. You *can* customize the templates, but you don't need to know any tech jargon to get started.

Advantages of domain-hosted blog host platforms

- Easy set-up: Your blog can be up and running in a matter of minutes.
- Features are easy to use: If you get stuck, tutorials are offered on each site and cover every blog set-up and management subject imaginable.
- Automatic updates: If there are changes to the platform, they happen automatically behind the scenes.

Wordpress.org is the self-hosted version of WordPress. This type of platform is best for bloggers who are very comfortable with technology.

Design Sponge Online is a self-hosted blog owned by Grace Bonney. She uses wordpress.org software for her blog that is dedicated to home and product design.

blogger.com

Blogger/Blogspot is a great blog host for the beginning blogger. Their tutorials are easy to follow and your blog can be up and running in minutes.

Kasey Buick's blog, Lola B's Boutique, is hosted by Blogger/Blogspot. She has personalized many elements of her blog, from the sidebar to the background.

Disadvantages of domain-hosted blog platforms

- Limited customization and design: You cannot configure your blog beyond set parameters.
- URL: Your URL is not truly unique; it will contain the name of the domain host along with your blog name. It will be something like: your blogname.yourbloghostname.com.
- Lack of control: You do not have ultimate control of your blog. Though you own the content, you do not own the URL, so moving your blog can present problems. Will readers be able to find you easily if you need to move your blog?

Choosing a Parking Place

Picking out your parking place on the Web is a very personal choice. Most creative bloggers use developer-hosted software platforms. For this reason, in this book we will talk about working with the top three platforms of this type: Blogger/Blogspot, WordPress, and TypePad. Keep in mind, though, that there are many other developer-hosted software programs available including AOL Journals, Google Live Pages, Tumblr, Vox, LiveJournal, and Xanga. You may want to visit a few of the sites before deciding on a platform. Each platform has its advantages and disadvantages and different factors to consider. All blogs have their own personal style and uniqueness. What may work for others may not work for you. Finding your comfort level and how you want your blog to appear will take a little time.

Blogger/Blogspot

Blogger/Blogspot is free. Developed by Pyra Labs and now owned by Google, this blog software includes it all: the platform, a Web address unique to you (blogname.blogspot.com), and hosting. A recent change in this service is that they now allow blog authors to easily customize their blog templates. A drag-and-drop feature lets you decide exactly where posts, profiles, archives, and other parts of your blog should appear on the page. It also has the ability to be private and viewed only by people you invite.

Amy Ockert from Bunny Rose Cottage (bunnyrosecottage.blogspot. com) shared her thoughts about creating her blog. When asked why she chose Blogger/Blogspot, she replied, "I had been a lurker of blogs for a while and was so impressed that I decided to start my own. Most of the blogs I visited were on Blogspot, so that is what I decided to try." Amy went on to say, "It was free to set up, which I was really pleased about, and I was surprised at how easy Blogspot was to work with. It is basically a form to fill out—and it sets the blog up for you." Other features Amy likes about Blogger/Blogspot include: ease of set-up and lots of add-ons, such as being able to link to favorite websites, stores, and blogs, or adding a poll or slide show in a post.

Barbara Jacksier from barbarajacksier.blogspot.com also had a few things to say about working with Blogger/Blogspot: "Rearranging page elements and making changes to features like About Me or My Beautiful Blogs links is a snap. Monitoring comments is simple; you just click on Publish or Reject. However, sometimes you are asked to sign in again, even if you already *are* signed in. The frequency that Blogger/ Blogspot asks you to sign in seems random and annoying. My main peeve with Blogger/Blogspot is how time-consuming it is to place photos into the text."

TypePad

TypePad is a paid blog software platform. Once you sign up, your blog address will be yourblogname.typepad.com. They offer hundreds of template designs, and these templates can be changed whenever you desire.

Hundreds of templates are provided by TypePad, and they can be customized to fit your needs.

Daisy Cottage is the TypePad-hosted blog belonging to Kim McCole. Her sunny images and positive and often funny stories warmly welcome visitors all year long.

typepad.com

$14.95 per month **TypePad Pro**
Take advantage of our comprehensive tools
professional bloggers.

- Create unlimited blogs mapped to your own doma
- Create collaborative blogs with guest authors
- Use advanced templates for complete control over designs
- 1 GB storage and 10 GB bandwidth per month
- $14.95/month or $149.50/year (save over 15%)

	Basic	Plus
Monthly subscription	$4.95	$8.95
Annual subscription — Get two months free!	$49.50	$89.50
	Sign Up	Sign Up
Find the answers you need		
Enjoy professional service and support	✓	✓
Gain access to priority support		
Create your blog and publish your content		
Create a blog	1	Up to 3
Create photo albums	Unlimited	Unlimited
Designate blog authors	1	1
Edit in Rich Text Format with spellcheck capability	✓	✓
Post by email or mobile device	✓	✓
Create audio and video podcasts	✓	✓
Enable RSS feeds	✓	✓
Map your blog URL to your domain name		✓
Schedule posts for future dates		✓
Customize your blog design		
Choose from professionally-designed templates	✓	✓
Drag and drop to customize layouts		✓
Customize any or all design elements using CSS and Advanced Templates		
Manage your blog content		

TypePad's various service levels offer many different features, from simple one-author posting to blogs that offer drag-and-drop customization features and podcasting abilities, to business blogs with multiple authors.

Widgets that can be added to your blog allow you to do things like play music, send text messages, view news headlines, and more. Adding things like images, blogrolls, even photo galleries can easily be done.

TypePad has a great feature that enables users to "pre-schedule" a post. If you are going to be out of town, you can set a post to go live while you are away, which lets you keep your readers entertained—and lets you avoid putting up the "closed for vacation" sign. This is a great feature for those on the move a lot. It also has a convenient comment feature that allows you to see the IP address of the commenter and provides a way to block the address, which comes in handy if they are a spammer or a negative Nancy who drops by to be mean. TypePad offers the most customization options of the three platforms featured in this book.

TypePad has been my host of choice for several years. When I started my blog in 2004 with a different host, I noticed that all the blogs I read frequently had TypePad in their URL address. I thought these blogs were so fresh, crisp, creative, and inspiring. There is an uncomplicated ease about the general set-up, and the new Compose Editor has made posting sheer heaven. TypePad even re-sizes my photos. Learning all the features took some time, but overall I am really happy with TypePad.

TypePad offers four tiers of services, so check out each before you choose what's right for you. For the beginning blogger, the Basic level provides just enough to get you started—one blog with plenty of designs to choose from. The Plus level gives you a couple of blogs, more storage, and the ability to use domain mapping. The Pro level doubles everything offered in the Plus level, and offers features that let you get more creative and have more control. With this service level, you can totally customize your blog's design, set up an unlimited number of blogs, and sign up as many authors as you'd like. With the Business Class service, you get all the features of Pro, plus unlimited storage and additional behind-the-scenes blog-management capabilities.

WordPress

While wordpress.org provides free blogging software for self-hosted blogs, wordpress.com is a free blog hosting platform and is what I will now refer to simply as WordPress. Once you sign up, your blog address will be yourblogname.wordpress.com. In addition to blog hosting, WordPress offers automatic software upgrades, support forums, comment tracking, and more.

More than 60 templates are available and you can switch them at the touch of a button. Several themes allow for the addition of a custom banner. You can have a blog up and running in minutes. A drag-and-drop feature lets you easily move around sidebar widgets. A built-in program blocks spam comments and spam trackbacks, and private blogs are available. Paid upgrades give authors more control over the look of their blog and more storage.

Claudia Strasser from The Paris Apartment (parisapartment.wordpress.com) has this to say about her current blog host: "Regarding WordPress, it is free so I have no idea why it hasn't caught on like Blogger/Blogspot and TypePad. When I first started, I opened accounts on both of those, too. In the end I chose the one that was the easiest for me to work with—Word-Press. It has great tracking, stats, links, and search words for your blog, along with a really simple format. I do think WordPress's templates are a little static and feel Blogger and TypePad offer more creativity on the design; however, I love working with WordPress because I wanted something super easy, without the glitches that I found on Blogger and TypePad."

No matter what service you choose in the beginning, it is possible to switch hosts down the road. The biggest blogging mistake I made was deleting my Blogspot blog, instead of transferring it to TypePad. I lost three years of my blog life. I've spoken with others who have done the same. It's like throwing away a journal by accident, watching it being taken away in the garbage truck, and running down the street after it in a robe and pink fuzzy slippers. Too late. It's gone.

WordPress templates feature clean and simple designs. Sidebar widgets can be changed on every template, and a few allow custom banners or backgrounds.

Claudia Strasser's blog is hosted by WordPress. She has taken advantage of many of WordPress's features to add links and images to her blog.

One reason I love photo banners is that they are easy to change. I swap out photos for the seasons, holidays, or for no reason at all.

Claire Robinson's unique graphic banner is the perfect topper to her blog, where she discusses everything from business to family and favorite things.

Amy Powers' blog, InspireCompany, has a clean graphic feel. Her simple banner sets the tone for what readers will see.

If you do decide to switch hosts, you don't need to make the same mistake I did. You can either bring your old posts over to your new blog, or create a link on your new blog that directs people to your old blog (this is called domain mapping). Each blog host has a tutorial on how to do this. Simply go to your blog's home page or dashboard and then click on FAQs, Help Desk, Help Center, or a similar link to find answers to your questions.

Basic Building Blocks

There are a few must-haves for every successful blog: a banner, a profile, and an email address for contact. These are the things that make your blog unique. Most blogs contain two or three columns. The main column usually takes up the most space on the page and is where blog posts are displayed. The remaining column(s) are called sidebars. Though not every blog has to have a sidebar, the majority of creative bloggers do use them.

A banner is located at the very top of a blog and contains the name of the blog. It can be something simple, like the name of your blog, or it can have a background such as a photograph or illustration. A banner doesn't have to be fancy or sparkly, but should represent you and your style.

Your profile, or About Me page, is where you introduce yourself to your readers. In general, people want to know three things: your name, where you live, and what your craft or passion is. You will need to decide how much information you are comfortable with divulging.

Readers want to know how to contact you. They may want to say thank you, or ask a question too personal for the comment section, or they may even be a long-lost friend. The philosophy of blogging and social networking has evolved over the years. Where you once were unsure about letting anyone out there on the World Wide Web know anything about you, blogging and other types of social networking sites like Facebook and MySpace have ushered in a new era of communication. Think of your blog as a new way to talk to others and make friends. You never know what message may be waiting for you or who you may meet. I remembered the editors of one of my favorite magazines and when I conceived the idea for this book, I used my blog to reach out to them.

Your blog's sidebar(s) is where things like links to your profile, photo galleries, blogrolls, archives, ads, feeds, and more are placed.

Where to Go for Help

The first place you should go for help is your blog's home page or dashboard. There you will find links to information and advice offered by your blog host. You will find information on everything from how to add a picture to a post to how to change the color of text on your blog, or add links and text.

Blog hosts also have forums where bloggers can post questions that will be answered by other bloggers, and help desks where bloggers can post questions that will be answered directly by a member of the blog host's support team.

If you are not satisfied with what you find on your host's site, then search the Internet. Whether you need help to figure out how to customize a background, resize images, or add music or video to your blog, simple searches will yield a multitude of answers. It will take time to comb through the answers to find what you need, but if you are patient the answers are out there.

If you see something you love on someone else's blog, like a banner or background, consider contacting the blog's owner and asking them how you can create something similar for your own blog. Still need help? Then it's time to call in either a tech-savvy friend who can help you for free, or pay a blog designer to do what you need.

On my About Me page I share details about all facets of my life, from where I grew up to stories about my husband and children, and a list of favorite things.

Alicia Paulson's pretty About Me page tells readers about her creative passions and her wildly successful business, Posie: Rosy Little Things.

TRACY PORTER: Tracy Porter Blog—Be Inspired

Find her: tracyporter.com/blog

Blogs about: decorating, DIY projects, entertaining, shopping

Tracy Porter, a mega brand name and popular designer of tableware, jewelry, and home accessories, joined the blogging scene in 2007. Her designs can be found throughout the globe. But Tracy, who hails from Wisconsin, says her goal is to be able to connect in a real way with her customers, let them understand that she is not just a big soulless corporation. "There is someone home, this is really who I am," she says. "I am not inventing a lifestyle, but living it daily."

Her video blog posts are incredibly fun and inspiring. Tracy takes you behind the scenes of her studio, home, and even catalog photo shoots. Her company is a 17-year-old brand with a very strong perspective on home and fashion; she tries to keep it real and personal with customers and readers.

It's important to her that she makes the reader want to come back for more, whether it's for more inspiration, to shop, or just to "hang out." Whatever the reader gets from Tracy's blog is good with her.

Tracy says her blog has definitely helped her business as she's watched her blog readership grow, but she won't let her blog "own her." She says, "I blog because I want to, not because I have to."

Tracy advises anyone starting a blog to do it because you love it, or because you need to grow your business and want to connect. Still, be prepared to walk away and not let the blog readers get too pushy. "It can be very demanding and you have to remember that you have a life and other realities," Tracy says. "Have a goal, be honest, and evaluate your traffic."

A few fashion tips for a smashing holiday!

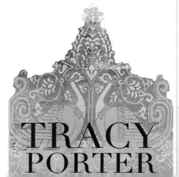

SERENA THOMPSON & TERI EDWARDS: The Farm Chicks

Find them: thefarmchicks.typepad.com

Blog about: business, cooking, crafting, motherhood, travel

For being new kids on the blogs, The Farm Chicks pretty much crossed the road and kept on running. This ultra dynamic duo, Serena Thompson and Teri Edwards, decided to start blogging recently to reach out to their readers in a more personal way. They hope to show that their lives of simplicity are meaningful and other mothers can follow their dreams.

These two stay-at-home moms started a business based on their love of old farms. Starting with a small online boutique, the business grew to encompass cooking and crafting as well. Today, these moms are superstars: they are contributing editors for "Country Living" magazine, host an annual antique fair, and have their own line of products including jewelry, clothing, and stationery. Their first book, entitled "The Farm Chicks in the Kitchen: Live Well, Laugh Often, Cook Much," was released in April 2009.

"Since we were new to the blog scene we have faced some challenges, especially on the technical side," Serena says. "Learning the ropes of a new program can be frustrating." Still, they are happily muddling through it because of the incredible support they received almost immediately. This new blog adventure has already taught them that if they work hard enough, they can accomplish anything.

The Farm Chicks plan to blog daily or at least several times a week and their hope is to grow their already booming business and reach out to others who haven't heard of them before. Their goal is to provide content they know their readers will enjoy, including recipes, projects, tips, things they love, and behind-the-scenes snapshots of their work.

Serena and Teri's favorite daily reads: angrychicken.typepad.com, designmom.com, jordanferney.blogspot.com

the Farm Chicks
WEB JOURNAL

ABOUT THE FARM CHICKS ···· SHOP ···· OUR WEBSITE ···· EMAIL ············ thefarmchicks.typepad.com

Boot season!

Don't you just love boot season? I just recently replaced my old, well worn black boots for a new pair that I hope will last for a few good years. I tend to

CHRIS GLYNN: Lucy's Lounge at Tutti Chic

Find her: tuttichic.typepad.com
Blogs about: design, family, gardening, humor

Grab some chocolate, kick up your heels, and enter the enchanted world of Lucy's Lounge—a creative, funny, and charming blog where owner Chris Glynn shares hilarious stories of her daily life. The owner of the popular online home décor boutique Tutti Chic also treats followers to glimpses of her elegant personal style, reflected in her stylish Massachusetts home.

This free spirit, talented artist, and avid gardener loves to laugh (and make others giggle with her), so naming her blog after her idol, Lucille Ball, was an easy choice. Images of 1950s Hollywood stars pair beautifully with vignettes of beautiful vintage décor on the banner and home page, making Tutti Chic a great blog for sopping up design ideas.

Chris has created the perfect recipe for her little nook on the Web, which includes inspiring design and garden ideas sprinkled with beautiful photography and a generous dash of humor.

Most posts relate to family life and Chris's passion for vintage romantic decorating. "I enjoy sharing the funny moments of my life, its ups and downs, both sad and happy times," she says. It's a combination that is a must-read for blog lovers. Her high energy and complete honesty makes her blog a popular daily stop for readers who admire her "Lucy-ness," as one reader puts it.

Chris enjoys how blogging allows her to connect with people around the world who share her similar passions. It's safe to say that when you enter Chris's blog, it's like entering Lucy Ricardo's 1950s apartment—you never know what she's up to next.

Chris's favorite daily reads: bellapink.typepad.com, sadieolive.typepad.com, teresaksheeley.typepad.com

ALYS GEERTSEN: Paris Couture Antiques

Find her: pariscoutureantiques.blogspot.com

Blogs about: antiques, business, everyday life, family, friends

Like many others, Alys Geertsen, owner of the online boutique, Paris Couture Antiques, began her blog as an extension of her shop. Because her shop is online only, and her customers span the globe, Alys found it hard to show off her personality and charisma in her boutique. At the time, she enjoyed looking at blogs and realized that starting one of her own was the answer. Her blog allowed her personality to shine through. Establishing friendships and a rapport with her customers is very important to her. Over time, her blog has evolved to encompass not just shop announcements, but her personal life as well.

"I treasure most the personal friends and colleagues I've met through blogging," Alys says. She loves the creative and therapeutic outlet that blogging provides, and is thrilled to receive feedback and comments. She has had the opportunity to reconnect with old friends with whom she had lost touch. Alys enjoys going back over her entries to see her growth, goals met, and the documentation of the path and journey she is on. Alys jokes that when she looks at her hairstyle from just one year ago, she knows that she has made good progress there, too.

Her advice is to find blogs that you enjoy reading and leave comments; let the blogger know what you like. "Set aside a couple of hours to allow yourself to get "lost" in the blogging world," Alys advises. Sit down and find yourself a good blog and look at the blogroll of other links to blogs, click around from blog to blog, take in the world of beautiful photos and wonderful writing, and you just might meet people and establish long-term friendships.

Alys' favorite daily reads: parishotelboutique.blog spot.com, parisapartment.wordpress.com, theoldpaint edcottage.blogspot.com

Find her: willows95988.typepad.com

Blogs about: French antiques, home décor, life in France

Tongue in Cheek is a beautiful blog written by Corey Amaro, an American living in France. She met her French husband 20 years ago in San Francisco. He spoke little English and she spoke even less French, but that didn't stop "l'amour" from blossoming. They've been together ever since.

Early in their marriage, the couple couldn't afford much in the way of housing. "Our first apartment was tiny, without any of what I like to call 'feather fluff,' " Corey recalls. This ignited a flea market passion, and Corey began transforming the tiny space into a cozy, feathered nest.

Her blog was started in 2005 on a dare by a friend, who encouraged her to write about her French flea market finds. Never one to shy away from a dare, Corey took the challenge and her blog was born. Her friend is responsible for the name, Corey says, since she considers Corey's style of French antiques "Tongue in Cheek"—serious but not stuffy, broken but still standing, original but not Monet. Corey hasn't missed a single day in her daily postings, an expectation she put on herself from the beginning. "I'm crazy and passionate like that—it's just the kind of person I am," she explains.

Over the years Corey has developed a talent for photography and shares her best secret: When you see a photo that you love, try to take one just like it. "An art teacher told me that and it was the best advice I ever got," Corey says.

While Tongue in Cheek is an intriguing name, Corey is one who wishes she had given her blog name more thought. "Tongue in Cheek sounds like a medical comedy," she laughs. So, when you visit Tongue in Cheek, just imagine that it's called "Petites Choses" (Little Things) and you'll feel right at home.

Corey's favorite daily reads: nieniedialogues.blogspot.com, ullam.typepad.com

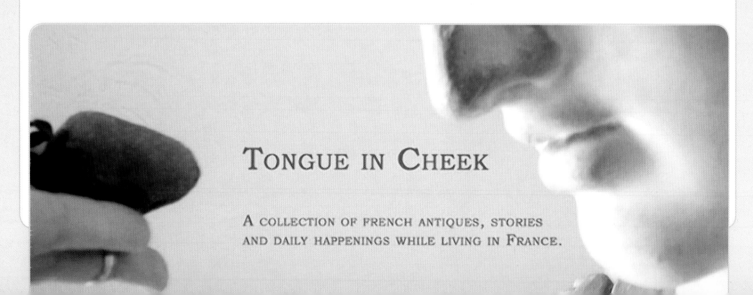

TONGUE IN CHEEK

A COLLECTION OF FRENCH ANTIQUES, STORIES
AND DAILY HAPPENINGS WHILE LIVING IN FRANCE.

Find her: shabbyfufu.blogspot.com
Blogs about: business, design, home décor

For veteran store owners like Janet Coon, a blog is the next logical step to giving their longtime customers just one more thing to love. "My customers were always begging me for decorating advice and photos of my home," says Janet, a home design expert, entrepreneur, writer, and antiques collector. "With a blog, I can do that."

Janet recognized early on the promise of online retailing. Her website, Shabbyfufu.com, showcases artisans who create one-of-a-kind products. Janet's specialty is stunningly embellished dress forms; she also helps her husband create teacup chandeliers, which are snapped up almost as fast as they can make them.

Janet absolutely loves blogging and only wishes she'd done it sooner. "It puts such a personal stamp on someone like me who runs a business," she says. "I get to meet the artisans who I've admired for so long. Turns out they're just ordinary people, although some of them live extraordinary lives."

Although she has become a blog junkie, Janet is very disciplined in her approach. She limits her time to one hour per post, and she sticks to a schedule. There is one mid-week "musing," a Friday shop talk, and then one additional post during the weekend, time permitting. She makes sure to include images of all of her projects and favorite finds in her posts. "I try to do my recreational surfing in the evenings, for relaxation," Janet says.

With her blog in full swing, Janet can now share the color palette of Florida that she loves so much with an even bigger audience. "You can't see the shop owner of an online boutique, but a blog turns you into a real person," she says. "It's made the world a more cozy space for me, knowing that there are others who care about how I feel and what I do."

Janet's favorite daily reads: deardaisycottage.typepad.com, gailmccormack.blogspot.com, mypetitemaison.blogspot.com

Shabbyfufu
Romantic Home & Garden Decor

Find her: thehappyzombie.com/blog
Blogs about: adventures, creativity, friends, life, quilts, stitchery

When Monica Solorio-Snow began her blog, she was hoping to have fun and to surround herself with like-minded, creative, happy people. Her expectations could not have been better met. She says, "Blogging has opened my eyes, and I see the world differently. I see beauty in things I would have never noticed pre-blogging. Even though I probably only blog one percent of the magic around me or the beauty before my eyes, I still feel and experience wonderment as if it's food for my blog, and that is magical to me."

Happy Zombie is Monica's second blog. Her first blog, Cheese Zombie, focused on politics, social issues, taxes, and similar subjects. But she wasn't happy. "After a while, I got tired of posting negative thoughts, as well as receiving negative and heated comments," she says.

While blog surfing one day, she came across some crafting and quilting blogs. "It was a happy, new, magical, and creative world I had discovered," she says. "I wanted to be a happy blogger, too."

Monica credits her love of cheese zombies and zombie-themed things like movies and dolls for inspiring her blog's unusual name. "Cheese zombies are a cafeteria staple in many California public schools, and one of my favorite foods when I was young," she says. "It's a fresh-baked bun filled with cheddar cheese."

When asked if she would consider having ads on her blog, Monica replies, "My blog is pure personal expression. I sell nothing and have no ads. I'm not opposed to blogs that sell, and I'm glad they do (I'm a shopper). It's just not for me." She doesn't have a business, but says, "Blogging has helped me network in the quilting and textile industry. Some of the freelance work I've done was a direct result of my networking through blogging."

Monica has the following advice for anyone wanting to start a creative blog. "Don't be scared to jump in," she says. "Creative blogland is a happy, welcoming place. Be you. Be nice. Be taking lots of photos. Be a visitor. Be a commenter. Be inspiring, be inspired and be ready to be friends with many wonderful people."

Monica's favorite daily reads: pamkittymorning.blogspot.com, allsorts.typepad.com, liquidskyarts.com/liquidblog/blogger.html, blog.nbc.com/dwightsblog

Happy Zombie

Quilting + Crafting + Friends = Zombie Fun

Find her: happylovesrosie.blogspot.com

Blogs about: crafts, decorating, family, friends, life experiences

Happy Harris has a way with words. She writes as if she is talking to her best friend. Because of this gift of gab, she has created a warm and welcoming place where bloggers from around the world love to visit every day. "I just wanted to create a fun and happy atmosphere, and report on places I have visited and experiences I have had," she says. "I think my blog is now a fun, happy, and colorful place to be. Somewhere to escape to when you are feeling low or just fancy a chat."

Happy Loves Rosie is the perfect name for this upbeat blogger. "My nickname is Happy and my daughter's middle name is Rosie," says Happy. "The name was supposed to be Happy and Rosie. I am a typical English Rose and suffer from red rosy cheeks quite often. But when signing up for Blogger, I wrote Happy Loves Rosie and it has stuck ever since. Plus, it's so apt."

Creative and very fond of color, Happy enjoys crafting, decorating, and traveling and shares it all in her posts, to which she receives many comments. "Most of the time it is my home pictures that gals like. They like to see how I have put my home together and the items that I have picked up on my travels—antique and flea market finds, charity shop deals, etc."

Happy's biggest challenge has been the technical aspect of blogging. "Learning HTML coding has been difficult," she says. "But with the help of a blogging friend I have learned how to achieve my three-column blog and how to change the backgrounds."

When asked what the best part of blogging is, Happy says, "It makes me look at things differently, to see every angle to a story. I also wrote a post about my mother. It was good to write about the experience I had with her. It helped us to patch up our relationship, and this has enhanced my life in more ways than you could ever know."

For Happy, blogging is a good way to let off some steam. "Life can be stressful at times," she says. "Blogging is a good pressure valve in more ways than one."

Happy's favorite daily reads: prettyshabby.blogspot.com, sugarandmeringue.blogspot.com, recordtheday.blogspot.com

HAPPY

VIEW MY COMPLETE

PROFILE

43

Chapter 3

LEARNING THE ROPES

So you've chosen your blog host service and have a basic idea of how you want your blog to look. Now what? Starting a blog may seem like a scary thing. Questions may race through your mind. What do I do first? Do I have to be a great writer? I'm not comfortable with computer jargon—can I still have a blog? How do people link to each other? How do I make a picture the right size? How can I change the banner? How can I change the background?

Fortunately, setting up a basic creative blog is simple. In this chapter you will learn what you need to know to get going.

What Kind of Blogger Are You?

Knowing your level of technical skill and what you desire from your blog is key to enjoying the experience. The more bells and whistles you want, the more skill, time, and work building and maintaining your blog will require. Here are some things to think about before you get started.

Beginner user

You are comfortable with the basics. Turning on your computer, reading and sending emails, listening to music, and watching DVDs are all things that are easy for you to do. You like your simple-to-use point-and-shoot camera, but uploading images? That leaves you quaking in your boots every time. Installing software? Forget that! You love reading blogs, and can navigate through links and pages.

Leaving comments on your favorite blogs has been your way of being involved with blogging. Writing your own blog sounds fun, but oh-so-scary. Blogger/Blogspot or WordPress would be the best options for you—they are both free and getting started is super simple. Stick with a basic template, learn the ropes, settle in, and get comfortable. Every new skill you learn is going to feel like a victory.

Moderate user

You know your way around the keyboard, and may even have a love affair with your digital SLR camera. Writing documents, finding files on your computer or information on the Internet, adding new programs, even uploading and playing around with images are second nature to you.

Learning computer programming or building websites holds absolutely no interest for you, however. You have your limits. Reading blogs is one of your favorite activities and having your own is top on your list. If you have one already, you're looking to spice things up with a fancy banner or cool background. Any of the domain hosts can work well for you, but you may want to go with Blogger/Blogspot or TypePad since they offer more customization options. Before deciding on a blog host, investigate what each one has to offer, so you can choose your best fit. Once you go through the basic set-up, you can use their tutorials to help you customize your blog.

Advanced user

Techie is the word to describe you. Computers don't intimidate you, they inspire you. You're the first to check out new programs and love learning new tricks. You read blogs, no, you devour blogs. So many places to go, so many things to learn, so many people to meet. You most likely have a blog already. Now's the time to dig in and use all a blog host has to offer to help you transform your blog into something truly unique. You may want to build your brand.

If you use your blog as part of your business, you may need multiple blogs and unique email addresses assigned to each blog. TypePad would be a great choice for you. They offer varying levels of service; either the Premier or Pro levels would be a great choice as each one has vast customization offerings.

Blogology 101: The Set-Up

A universal experience of setting up and customizing your own blog seems to be a bit akin to driver training classes. Sooner or later you have to just get behind the wheel and learn to steer the car. The most popular blog platforms are always evolving. Because practice is the best teacher, I suggest that once you choose a host platform, you stick with the tutorials on its site until you feel comfortable with the basics you can learn there. Websites are constantly evolving, so by the time you visit these blog hosts, the pages may appear different. They will still contain the

Blogger/Blogspot

1 To get started on your Blogger/Blogspot blog, go to blogger.com. You will land on this start page. Click on the Create a Blog link to begin.

2 Create a Blogger account on this opening page. If you don't already have a free Google account, such as Gmail or Google Groups, you will need to create one as you will use it to sign in to Blogger. This is necessary because it is owned by Google.

necessary information. You will soon realize that there are as many ways of customizing and personalizing your blog as there are bloggers. You will find yourself visiting a blog and asking yourself, "How did she do that?" It's not difficult and remember, there are many places to go for help.

Design Sources

smittenblogdesignsgallery.blogspot.com
This site is hosted by two friends who must spend countless hours designing these free templates for Blogger users. They are wonderful, and include all the elements needed for a good blog as well as easy installation instructions.

3 Choose your blog title and enter it in the top box. The next box is where you will enter your desired URL (blog address). Click on the link to make sure your desired URL is available. If it isn't try again! Most often a simple change is all that's needed. The word verification is an example of CAPTCHA, and prevents fraud and spamming. If you have advanced needs, then check out those links. If not, click on the Continue button.

4 Choose your desired theme from the list of templates shown on this page. You can click on each template to view a larger version. Be mindful of the color schemes and choose something you will be comfortable working with.

youtube.com

YouTube has great tutorials on just about every aspect of working on a blog. Many of the videos available are even specific to a platform and the software you may own to work on a custom banner or background. I recommend the videos with narration. There are plenty available that will walk you through using a program such as Photo-Shop. Look for tutorials with high viewership and good ratings so you don't waste your time.

5 Your blog has been created! You can go straight to writing your first post, or you may choose to write your profile and customize your blog before going "live." The choice is up to you. You may want to take time to read through everything Blogger/Blogspot has to offer before jumping in.

6 The dashboard is where you control what happens with your blog. From here you can view and edit your profile and photo, change your settings and template, post, add blogrolls, images, and ads, and find answers to questions.

thecutestblogontheblock.com

The Cutest Blog on the Block has delightful blog designs you can download and customize for just a few dollars. The site includes an online community for exchanging ideas and has some great free tutorials. Just be careful, as some of the designs are busy, busy, busy and the background choices can make it very hard to read your blog entries. Sometimes more is more and not always good.

TypePad

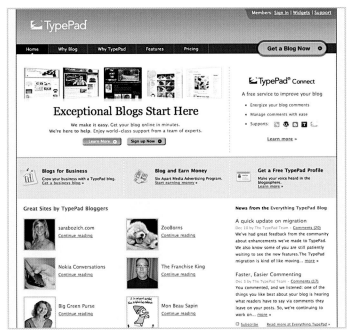

1 To get started on your TypePad blog, go to typepad.com. You will land on this start page. You can read about the different TypePad offerings, or click on the Get a Blog Now link to begin.

2 With TypePad, you create your blog account using an established email (it does not matter what email service you use). If you don't have an email address, you will need to create one. There are many free email services available including Hotmail, MSN, Gmail, Yahoo!, AOL Mail, and many more. Type in your desired blog address; you will be notified if it is not available. Check that you have read the Terms of Service then click on Create Your Account.

onecuteblog.blogspot.com

Now this extremely creative and generous soul has done lots and lots of work creating delightful backgrounds for free download. The author, Krista Arave, even provides very easy-to-follow instructions for installing them on your blog. All she asks in return is that you mention her and link back to her site. Kris does do custom work too, but it seems only fair that you pay her for anything over and above what she already generously supplies.

3 TypePad is a paid blog hosting service. You will need to choose what level of service you need. If you don't need any bells and whistles and do not want to customize your blog, choose TypePad Basic. If you want the ability to customize your banner and more, choose TypePad Plus. Business and professional bloggers should read though what is offered with TypePad Pro and TypePad Premium prior to making a choice about level of service. You will need to choose whether to pay monthly or annually and you are required to provide billing information.

4 Choose your blog title. You can change this at any time. Choose a layout. TypePad offers five different layout styles; each one varies in how the columns are displayed. Choose a theme. TypePad offers hundreds of standard themes and with each one you have a color choice. Many of the themes can be customized. Make sure to choose one that can be changed if you are planning to create a unique look for your blog.

eblogtemplates.com

This one-stop shop offers templates for Blogger/Blog-spot, TypePad, and WordPress. There are dozens of free templates available as well as premium templates that can be purchased. Templates are available in a wide range of styles and colors, from clean and contemporary to vintage. eBlog Templates also provides tutorials and videos on subjects including advertising, adding widgets, blog set-up, and search engine optimization.

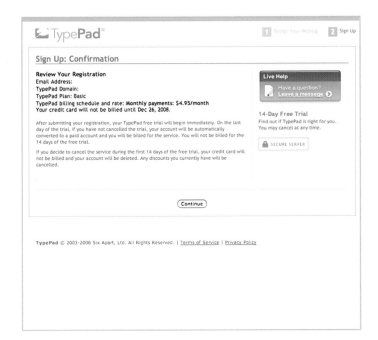

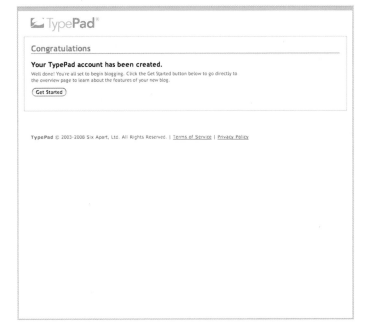

5 Confirm your order choices and press the Continue button. If you need to make any changes, press the back button on your browser. Once finished with this, you are now on your way!

6 Your account has been created. Click on the Get Started button to go to your blog's dashboard, where you can go straight to posting, read articles from TypePad's knowledge base; or customize your blog with photo albums, blogrolls, and more.

dailyblogtips.com

This website has some excellent links to freebie help and templates for WordPress users. Take a look at the article, "How to Dress Your Blog for Success." The links are at the bottom of the page and most of them are short and sweet.

becomeablogger.com

Okay, fair warning. This website is a little commercialized and they are trying to sell a book. If you decide that wordpress.org is the right choice for you, there is a series of 10 free instructional videos well worth watching.

• •

WordPress

1 To get started on your free WordPress blog, go to wordpress.com. You will land on this start page. Here you can read about WordPress, visit blogs, or click on the Sign Up Now! link to begin.

2 Set up your wordpress.com account. Choose your username and password. You must have a valid email account to sign up. Check the box that you have read through all of their legalese. (It's always a good idea to actually read it.) Choose the Gimme a Blog! button and click on the Next button.

bloggingthemes.com

Website has free blog themes for WordPress.

etsy.com

The Web home of all things handmade. Search for banner, template, or other blog elements to yield tons of results.

lenatoewsdesigns.blogspot.com

This site, Simply Fabulous Blog Templates, offers beautiful templates for use with Blogger/Blogspot. There are dozens of free templates available. Custom templates can be designed for a fee. Free tutorials offer advice on adding various elements to your blog.

3 Choose your blog's URL; choose wisely as this cannot be changed. Choose the title of your blog. This is what will appear at the top of your blog (the banner). Choose the language in which your blog will appear. Check the privacy box if you would like your blog to appear in search engines. Click on the Sign-Up button to continue to the next step.

4 Your account is set up and you are ready to start blogging on your WordPress blog. You will receive a confirmation email that you will have to answer before continuing. Once you reply to the email, you can log in to go to your blog's dashboard.

5 Your WordPress blog's dashboard has links to the places where you can control the look of your blog, write and edit posts, and more. The QuickPress section allows you to post to your blog directly from this page. You can even manage incoming links, comments, and upgrades to your account.

When designing her blog Artsy Mama, Kari Ramstrom made sure to customize her banner and background. Her blog is visually full and stunning.

Tracy Porter created an awesome video about decorating for the holidays and posted it on her blog. This is a great way to keep readers interested.

Getting Started

Once you decide on a hosting service, you can go straight to writing your first post, or you can take some time to include basic features on your blog such as a banner, or sidebar elements like your profile.

Visit your blog's home page or dashboard and choose what elements you would like to work on. Your profile is a must, so why not start there? If you blog for bliss, letting folks know your full name and location isn't important; however, do share things like your interests and passions, your family (you don't have to include names), what you do for fun, and why you blog. You can divulge as much or as little as you desire. Keep in mind that the information, stories, and images you share on your blog are there for the whole world to see. Be careful not to share information that could be used by unscrupulous characters. Many bloggers choose not to share family names or direct contact information. If you blog for business, it is important and advantageous to let folks know about your business and how to reach you.

If you want to use a simple text banner as provided in your basic blog set-up, you will find information about adding one on the blog home page or dashboard. You will learn how to create a custom banner in Chapter 4.

Adding links and categories to your sidebar(s) is simple, no matter what blog host platform you use. Again, go to your blog's home page or dashboard and click on the links provided to customize your sidebar. You can change around the features on your blog at any time, so don't stress about making your blog "perfect" right off the top. Your blog will evolve over time as your comfort and skill level increases.

Adding Music, Videos, and Podcasts

Including music, videos, or podcasts can add a dynamic look and feel to your blog. Blogger, TypePad, and WordPress all have widgets available to help you add these features. You will find links to widgets on your blog's dashboard.

The Write Stuff

A question on every blogger's mind is, "How do I write good posts?" Ask ten bloggers this question and you will get ten different answers. The most important advice is, again, write from your heart. Blissful bloggers connect to posts that tell a story. The story can be anything from what your preschooler said that morning to what craft project you are working on, or details about a special day with friends.

Before getting started with your first post, it's important to know what is included with your post once you publish it on your blog. Most blog posts will contain the following:

- The date the post was published.
- The time the post was published.
- A link to the permalink page for the post.
- A link to the category where the post has been placed.

Here are a few tried-and-true techniques to help you craft successful, enjoyable posts and keep your readers coming back for more:

Read other blogs
Just like reading well-written books will help you improve your writing, reading enjoyable blogs will help you decide how to approach your own blog.

Take your time
Choose one subject to talk about in each post; this will make the experience more enjoyable for you and your reader. Need inspiration? Just look around. It could be just sitting there in a pile of fabric scraps. What were you working on? Where did you find the fabric? What do you love about it?

Put some effort into writing your titles
An interesting title draws your readers in and tells them what to expect. Search engines look at titles when searching for matches, so make sure your titles describe your posts.

Lisa Tutman Oglesby regularly features how-to projects on her blog. At the bottom of each post readers can click on links to see other posts in the same category.

With titles like "Adorned Cuff Bracelet," Andrea Singarelli's blog is clean and concise, making it easy for her readers to find content.

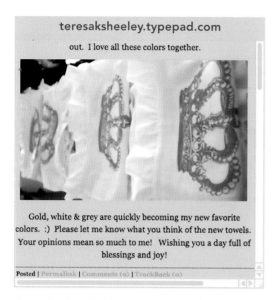

teresaksheeley.typepad.com

out. I love all these colors together.

Gold, white & grey are quickly becoming my new favorite colors. :) Please let me know what you think of the new towels. Your opinions mean so much to me! Wishing you a day full of blessings and joy!

Posted | Permalink | Comments (9) | TrackBack (0)

Teresa Sheeley asked for her readers' opinions about her new line of towels. This is a great way to get responses to your blog.

teresaksheeley.typepad.com

Just wanted to pop in and say how sweet you girls are that you love the tea towels!! I was a little nervous about how they would go over, but you have given me confidence and a smile. Okay so now to let you know about shipping, etc.

She asked and her readers responded. Teresa Sheeley thanks readers for responding to her question about her tea towels in this post on her blog.

Write short paragraphs

There is no rule about how long paragraphs should be, but keep in mind that blog readers have a tendency to scan anything that is too long.

Use spell check

Readers appreciate good writing, so make sure to check your spelling and use proper grammar.

Post pictures

Creative bloggers love to be inspired visually, so make sure to include at least one image in every post. The image may inspire what you write about.

Use interesting fonts

Formatting such as bold and italics help emphasize your points, just don't go overboard. A little goes a long way.

Leave some breathing room

Don't feel like you have to fill every single inch of space on your computer screen. Create posts that make your readers feel welcomed, not overwhelmed, by too many distractions.

Ask for input

When you share an experience, ask readers their thoughts on the subject. Have they gone through a similar experience? Do they have any suggestions?

Write a Top 10 list

Then ask readers to share their favorites on the subject.

Be obvious

Make sure that the Leave Comment button is easy to find and use.

Be on time

Respond to comments in your next post.

Blog Speak

Many of us use shortcuts in life, such as a quicker way to the market or running up the steps instead of waiting for the elevator. So why not use some shortcuts on your blog? While not everyone knows "blog speak" or "text talk," many acronyms are gaining in popularity. I emailed my sister once and wrote "LOL." She immed-iately emailed me back and asked, "Who is LOL?" When I told her it meant "Laughing Out Loud" she typed back "Oh! I always wondered why everyone was talking about LOL [as if it were a person]."

Here are some fun "blog speak" terms you may encounter, or just enjoy using:

BRB	Be right back	ONNA	Oh, no, not again
BTW	By the way	OTOH	On the other hand
C U L8R	See you later	OTTOMH	Off the top of my head
IMHO	In my humble opinion	PLS	Please
IMNSHO	In my not so humble opinion	POV	Point of view
IMO	In my opinion	RHB	Read his/her blog
IRL	In real life	ROTF	Rolling on the floor
IYKWIM	If you know what I mean	ROTFL	Rolling on the floor laughing
JIC	Just in case	ROTFLOL	Rolling on the floor laughing out loud
JK	Just kidding	RSN	Real soon now
KISS	Keep it simple stupid	RTD	Read the directions
L8TR	Later	RUOK	Are you okay?
LOL	Laughing out loud	SOL	Smiling out loud
LTNS	Long time no see	TAFN	That's all for now
MOL	More or less	THX	Thanks
MTCW	My two cents' worth	TIA	Thanks in advance
NRN	No reply necessary	UMO	Unwarranted Music Onslaught
OIC	Oh I see	W/	With
OMG	Oh my gosh	WTG	Way to go

Kari Ramstrom created a numbered list of things to do on her blog, Artsy Mama. Lists are a great way to attract readers to an interesting post.

Kim McCole used the headline "Happy December!" in her post that thanked readers for reading with her blog.

Simple Codes

What is HTML? It is the code that tells your browser all sorts of things, like where to find images, how text is supposed to look, and where links on your page go to. You don't need to know what HTML is or how to use it to have a blog. However, you can give your blog a little bit of pizzazz without getting code overload; you only need to know a few of the basics.

Before using any of the codes shown here, check your blog's knowledge base. Your blog host may have preferred ways to add HTML code to blogs hosted on their site.

HTML code is simple to use. Each host service gives access to at least a bit of code. Usually there is a button like "Edit HTML" located on the page where you compose a post. Simply click on the button to view the HTML code for that page. There are a few basic HTML tags to learn to customize your blog.

Things you can change or add with HTML include banner colors, images, links, headings, font formatting, lists, and symbols. There is an opening tag (<>) and a closing tag (</>) for almost every code. The tags enclose the text or command; however, exceptions include the code used to insert line breaks.

Line breaks

To insert a line break, simply type in the code exactly where you want to include a blank space between lines.

```
CODE
<br>
```

Headlines

There are six levels of headlines that can be created with HTML. Each level headline represents a different size text.

Header tags are written like this:

CODE	ONLINE VIEW
<h1>Headline 1</>	**Headline 1**
<h2>Headline 2</>	**Headline 2**
<h3>Headline 3</>	**Headline 3**

Formatting text

You can change the look of your font with HTML. Emphasize text using bold, italics, and underline attributes. Make a paragraph stand out with the use of a block quote, which indents the text on the left and on the right.

- To bold text:

CODE	ONLINE VIEW
This text is bold.	**This text is bold.**

- To italicize text:

CODE	ONLINE VIEW
<i>This text is italicized.</i>	*This text is italicized.*

- To underline text:

CODE	ONLINE VIEW
<u>This text is underlined.</u>	This text is underlined.

Lidy Baars adds interest to the look of her blog, French Garden House, by using different sizes of text in each post.

Sandra Evertson uses a line break between images on her blog. This gives center stage to her pictures.

donnaobrien.typepad.com

THE SPECIAL EFFECTS: *Embellished Antiqued Mirrors.*

Donna O'Brien used bold letters and italics to add interest to her post about one of her creations.

blessedanddistressed.blogspot.com

Coming Together

This past fall I stopped by my local antique mall near my work, and found 3 drawers that were on sale... marked down to $4.00 a piece! I knew that they would be the perfect addition to my studio turned on edge to create shelving on the wall.

Sheila Rumney used the headline "Coming Together" for a post about decorating with antiques.

- To create a block quote:

CODE
`<blockquote>The text within these tags will be indented on the left and on the right. </blockquote>`

ONLINE VIEW
The text within these tags will be indented on the left and on the right.

Lists are an easy way to create an interesting post. Adding them through the use of HTML is easy. Two of the simplest lists are an unordered list, which appears as a bulleted list, and an ordered list, which appears as a numbered list.

- To create an unordered list:

CODE	ONLINE VIEW

`<ul>`
  `<li>Apple Pie</li>`
  `<li>Blueberry Pie</li>`
`</ul>`
	• Apple Pie
	• Blueberry Pie

- To create an ordered list:

CODE	ONLINE VIEW

`<ol>`
  `<li>First Item</li>`
  `<li>Second Item</li>`
`</ol>`
	1. First Item
	2. Second Item

I'm often asked how to put symbols within a post. Here is the code to use to add some common symbols:

- To add a trademark symbol:

CODE	ONLINE VIEW
&trade	™

- To add a copyright symbol:

CODE	ONLINE VIEW
&copy	©

- To add an ampersand:

CODE	ONLINE VIEW
&amp	&

There will be times when you'll want readers to be able to link to a Web page as they read your post. Here is how you do it:

- To link to a Web page:

CODE
<a href="http://www.maryellensblog.com/"> Visit Mary Ellen's blog </a>

ONLINE VIEW
Visit Mary Ellen's blog

There are multitudes of things you can do with HTML code. Your host platform will offer tutorials on using HTML on your blog.

This quote from Jennifer Perkins of the Naughty Secretary Club is a great example of a block quote. The red text helps it stand out even more.

On her blog, Vintage Indie, Gabreial Wyatt regularly links to other blogs as seen in this post about Heather Bullard's Vintage Living.

Webspeak

Acquiring new computer skills, including blogging, can make you feel like you're learning a new language. And to a certain degree, you are. In order to feel comfortable in this new venture, there are a few terms you will need to know. The following is a limited list of phrases and terms that you will come across as you set up your blog, and read or write posts. On the facing page you see an illustration of where each phrase is located on a typical blog. An extended Glossary of blog and Web terms can be found on page 148.

Building Your **Blog**

1. **Blog:** Short for weblog; a website that is an online journal with interactive features.

2. **Address bar:** This is the input box at the top of the browser window that shows the URL (internet location) of the current Web page you are viewing.

3. **Banner:** Decorative horizontal space at top of page where blog name is displayed.

4. **Title:** The name of a post.

5. **Reciprocal links:** Links posted on one's blog to other bloggers.

6. **Tags:** Simple category names. Bloggers can categorize their posts, images, and more with any tag they think makes sense.

7. **Comment:** A response written by a reader to a blog post. Comments are the interactive feature that makes blogs different than a static Web page.

8. **Template:** Blog presentation design.

9. **Sidebar:** One or more columns along one or both sides a blog's main page.

10. **Profile:** Information contained on a blog about the blog owner. Usually accessed by a clickable link found on the blog home page. Includes the blogger's name, contact information, hobbies, career, passions, and likes and dislikes.

11. **Categories:** Links on a blog sidebar that contain similar types of posts. Categories help readers find posts you've written on general topics.

12. **Archives:** A collection of all previous posts on one page. Can be categorized by month, year, etc.

13. **RSS Feed:** RSS (Real Simple Syndication) is a format for delivering regularly updated Web content. Visitors to your blog can click on the RSS Feed link and they will automatically be notified when your blog is updated.

1

2

Daily Courage

http://www.redlips4courage.com/dailycourage/ • Google

8

3

daily Courage

4 Crowns and Tiaras

9

Welcome!

I'm Eileen Paulin, a mother, a wife and Custodian of a creative services company named Red Lips 4 Courage Communications, Inc.

10 *About Me*

Categories

11
- » Artists We Love
- » Blogging
- » Crowns
- » Crowns & Tiaras
- » Decor
- » Designers We Love
- » Fiber Arts
- » Four Paws - Cats & Dogs
- » General Courage

5 Our special thanks on behalf of the authors to the wonderful artists who made the magic happen. Pam Garrison created the incredible crown in the above shot. While we were working on the book, our friend Judy Watkins, www.remnantofthepast.com, lost her mother after a long battle with cancer. Placing Pam's crown upon her head the day of the funeral brought a smile to Judy's face and reminded her that, *"Everyone is the Queen of Something."*

12

Previous Posts

- » November
- » September
- » August

Feeds

13
Bloglines

6 Posted in Tiaras, Vintage jewelry, Crowns, Crowns & Tiaras, Jewelry

7 1 Comment »

JANE GOBLE: Posy

Find her: posy.typepad.com

Blogs about: English countryside, florals, personal, vintage finds

Jane Goble, from a little town in Devon, England, hosts a lovely blog admired by creative souls from around the globe. She began her blog in 2006 and named it Posy because of her love of florals (coincidentally, it's the name of her cat, too).

Jane dove into the creative blog world because of a deep desire to share her loves and passions. Also, her husband is from New Zealand and she thought the blog would be a wonderful way for his family to see what was going on in their lives. "I figured it would be a quick solution to my appalling lack of letter writing and regular correspondence," Jane says.

She admits her minimal computer knowledge made for a slow start, but she soon found that her gracious host at TypePad was very helpful; she also relied on her fellow bloggers to get the answers. Jane finds that the creative blogging community is always willing to share and help.

Jane blogs about anything inspiring, from the ordinary to the unexpected. She blogs about items found in her pursuit of all things floral and vintage: the beautiful English countryside; her latest craft project; and her love for her family, home, and amusing things that happen to her. Her posts are usually written around a photograph, so she keeps her camera with her at all times, and she loves to take snapshots of what seems to be odd things (for example, the tower of holiday magazines piled high in her shopping trolley—that's cart to those on the other side of the Pond).

Visit Posy for a good example of how to weave story threads throughout a blog. Jane's attempt to finish a crocheted blanket (and all the other unfinished pieces around her) is humorous and creates a compelling storyline that readers want to come back to, again and again.

Jane's favorite daily reads: attic24.typepad.com, rosehip.typepad.com, soulemama.typepad.com

SHEILA RUMNEY: Blessed and Distressed

Find her: blessedanddistressed.blogspot.com
Blogs about: creativity, family, friends, inspirations, mixed-media art, scrapbooking

Mixed-media artist and scrapbooker Sheila Rumney began her blog in April 2007 as a way to share information about classes she teaches at a local scrapbook store and to record, as she explains, "the blessings in my life, from my family and friends, to my artwork and antiques I find along the way." Now, after blogging for more than two years, Sheila describes her online journal as "a welcoming, positive place that I hope encourages others."

Blessed and Distressed seemed like the natural choice for Sheila when she was deciding on a blog name. "I came up with Blessed and Distressed as a way to define me and my personality," she says. "I have been blessed with a loving and supportive family, and I am a wife and mother to two beautiful children. I also love all things distressed, worn, and aged."

Sheila has found that blogging has impacted her life in many positive ways. "Blogging has given me the courage to meet and reach out to other incredibly talented women who share my passions," she reveals. "It has also reminded me that dreams do come true, with a little bit of courage, work, and tenacity. Without blogging I may have never been encouraged to make the jump into mixed-media art, where I find the greatest joy."

Like many bloggers, Sheila describes herself as technically challenged and says, "The biggest hurdle is trying to figure out how to achieve the look that I want for my blog, especially if it involves a lot of computer knowledge." When she does run into trouble, she reaches out to the blogging community for answers.

For anyone considering starting an online journal, Sheila has a few recommendations. "Check out some blogging magazines or articles to find the blogs that inspire you and speak to your heart," she advises. "Then blog hop using the blogrolls and links you find on those blogs. Through blogging, inspiration is shared and friendships are formed, and I believe the world is a little bit better for it."

Sheila's favorite daily reads: the-feathered-nest.blogspot.com, rebeccasower.typepad.com, romanticthoughtsfromalicew.blogspot.com, teresamcfayden.typepad.com

Blessed and Distressed
welcome...

distressed vintage with a shabby chic flair

KASEY BUICK: Lola B's Boutique

Find her: lolabboutique.blogspot.com

Blogs about: business, everyday life, home décor

Shop owner Kasey Buick's blog, Lola B's Boutique, is like a beautiful virtual vestibule just outside of her boutique in St. Charles, Illinois. Very often, visitors have seen a new item or a particularly dazzling display on the blog and then come to the store to see it for themselves.

This connection between the digital and the physical world has provided Kasey not only with a new circle of customers, but a great many new friends as well. "There's nothing more thrilling than to blog and then get such positive feedback," Kasey says. "I love my readers, and I love seeing their blogs as well."

She advises creative bloggers to always remember the importance of "eye candy"—make your blog as appealing as you can. Kasey does this by interspersing news about her family with little peeks inside her home, along with posts that chronicle what's going on in her shop. "Even if you are a business owner, make sure you reveal personal things, too," Kasey advises. "That way your customers will really feel like they know and trust you."

Kasey is living proof that bloggers are keeping watch on the world and aren't afraid to voice their opinions. Her photo essay on homes—going from a shack to grander-than-grand home, wondering which one we are wishing for, then showing a homeless family in their car who just wants the shack—is a heartfelt treat you don't want to miss.

"Blogging has taught me that I am creative, that I can take a great picture and do anything I set my mind to," Kasey says. "It was a lot of hard work getting my blog name out there, but I did it."

Kasey is moving her boutique out of town and into the barn behind her 100-year-old home in the country. She is relying on her blog and online retail shop to keep things going until she gets settled. Her virtual vestibule is warm, inviting, and always open.

Kasey's favorite daily reads: blissfulb.blogspot.com, mcmasterandstorm.blogspot.com, shoptalkbuzz.blogspot.com

LISA TUTMAN OGLESBY: Celebrate Creativity in all its forms

Find her: lisatutmanoglesby.typepad.com

Blogs about: baking, crafting, dollmaking, fellow bloggers, scrapbooking, stenciling

Lisa Tutman Oglesby has never met a craft she didn't like. This talented blogger does scrapbooking, photography, quilting, sewing, dollmaking, embroidery, baking, stenciling…and still finds time to run her magnificent blog. Besides her many creative talents, Lisa exudes a generous spirit and likes to lift up her fellow bloggers by offering advice, leaving comments on their blogs, and encouraging them to try her projects by providing lots of instruction and additional resources.

"It's very important to encourage other bloggers and recognize the effort they put into creating a post and offering it up for review," Lisa says. "This also helps create a sense of community, fellowship, and goodwill in the blogosphere." And at the risk of seeming too self-interested, it brings readers back to your blog as well.

After winning a national scrapbooking contest a few years ago, Lisa was busy posting her samples onto several scrapbooking magazine sites, but felt bad that she couldn't share photos and how-to instructions for her other creative work. That's when she decided to create a blog of her own. Lisa describes her blog as a colorful mix of craft projects and tutorials that touch on a bit of everything in the crafts world.

At first, Lisa was posting one project each week, complete with instructions. "The pace was difficult for me to maintain but I didn't want to disappoint my visitors who knew the schedule," Lisa explains. "Soon it was feeling much more like a chore and a lot less fun."

Lisa moved to a bi-monthly schedule, posting on the 1st and the 15th of every month so that everyone knows when to expect a new project. So far, the change has worked perfectly. Lisa loves the TypePad platform because it allows her to store multiple drafts and then publish them as needed. "Find the schedule that works best for you," she says. "If you are passionate about what you are posting, that will come through loud and clear."

Lisa's favorite daily reads: dubuhdudesigns.typepad.com, inkvanilla.typepad.com, moderncountry.blogspot.com, pintuckstyle.blogspot.com

celebrate CREATIVITY in all its forms

EMILY FLETCHER MOSS: Ravenhill

Find her: ravenhill.typepad.com

Blogs about: fabrics, Metroyshka dolls, motherhood, projects

In Norway during the winter, there are only a few hours of sunshine. That's why Oslo-based Emily Fletcher Moss has a little trick for taking her blog photos: "I have a light box that people use for Seasonal Affective Disorder in a pinch."

Emily has lots of tricks and ideas for Ravenhill, a blog named after the street where she lives. Her joy and creative talents pay off, as Ravenhill is a bright and cheerful blog filled with gorgeous Norwegian fabrics, stories about her children, a bit of embroidery, and of course her handmade Metroyshka dolls.

These nesting dolls are sold on Emily's Etsy site, so they're mainly for decoration and inspiration on the blog. Emily considers the materials of her craft beautiful in and of themselves—thread, fabric, trim, yarn, and other bits create vignettes as pretty as the finished projects. "I just have to share the beauty and endless possibilities of the latest finds, be it vintage velvet ribbons or a little pile of new Norwegian designer fabrics," she says.

Emily is grateful for the many like-minded artists she has met all over the world through her blog. She feels that owning a blog has made her a better crafter, photographer, designer, and writer. She tries to answer anyone who leaves a comment, although the task gets overwhelming at times. But the connection to other people is the most important reason Emily continues blogging. "I love the feeling of having just finished a post," she says. "Blogging has showed me that I may not be so good at doing things right away but with work I can get better."

At first, Emily blamed some of her not-so-great photos on her 3-year-old camera, but she's still using it. It's not the camera that takes bad pictures, she notes, it's the photographer. In the two years she's been blogging, Emily's photographs have improved tremendously. Just goes to show, good things come to those who practice.

Emily's favorite daily reads: erleperle.typepad.com, homespunliving.blogspot.com, moonstitches.typepad.com, spiritcloth.typepad.com

Find her: inspireco.blogspot.com
Blogs about: business, crafting, family, projects

Amy Powers started her blog in the summer of 2005. There weren't a whole lot of crafty bloggers back then and she thought it would be a good way to communicate with customers of her online boutique. Blogging seemed more personal and she liked the fact that customers could choose to read her blog, as opposed to the "in-your-face" aspect of mass emails.

Amy shares creative ideas and projects that hopefully inspire others. A self-proclaimed "ordinary girl, living a happy and ordinary life," Amy tries to see things in a positive light and faces challenges with a "How can I learn from this?" attitude.

She likes to think of her blog as a place to come for a bit of cheerful inspiration and project ideas. She shares information about her life when appropriate and readers really get to know her whole family by reading her posts. This includes Amy's 75-year-old father, who reads her blog faithfully. "My dad would never let me live it down if I tried to be someone I'm not," Amy laughs.

Amy's blog is a true reflection of her personality and her life. She writes exactly how she talks and shares details openly. Her entries are inspired as she goes through her day, always thinking of what is "bloggable," meaning, interesting to her readers. "People always come forward when I need a little pick-me-up or when I've written about things going not so well," says Amy. "When I posted about our decision to become foster parents and shared our fertility issues, I got a record number of comments...all of them wonderful and encouraging."

Amy's advice for those who are thinking of starting a blog is a few words from Shakespeare: "To thine own self be true." Don't try to copy what other folks are doing; make your own mark and help others learn more about you. "Jump in with both feet," Amy says. "The water's fine!"

Amy's favorite daily reads: redshoesllc.typepad.com, rosylittlethings.typepad.com, ullam.typepad.com

inspirecompany

shop blog magazine featured artist

follow the adventures of the gift fairy herself

CLAUDIA STRASSER: The Paris Apartment

Find her: parisapartment.wordpress.com
Blogs about: all things French, antiques, art, family, films, travel

Claudia Strasser took her first step towards her destiny in 1993, when she opened a little shop in the East Village of New York City. This lover of all things French—especially 18th-century French—dazzled fans with her refurbished boudoir furniture, chandeliers, textiles, and accessories. Two years later her book came out "The Paris Apartment: Romantic Décor on a Flea-Market Budget," along with oodles of press.

Claudia didn't discover blogging until two years ago—and feels that now, she has truly found her voice. "I love that blogs are sort of the modern-day 'salon' where conversations are ongoing," she says. "To publish something daily, weekly, anytime, is incredible."

Her longtime customers continue to relish her posts about French discoveries on her many trips abroad, but Claudia says she is writing for herself. She wants her posts to be fresh and authentic; punctuated, of course, with lots of fabulous photographs. In her posts, Claudia writes about a range of topics, from the history of her favorite artists to the architectural details of a vacation retreat.

Her sources are many. Besides her own boutique items, Claudia will post stills from a movie, shops that she likes, and anything else that's "Frenchy, pretty, or inspiring."

If a week goes by without a post, Claudia doesn't worry about it. Her primary focus is on the blogroll. "Make sure you have an interesting and varied blogroll," she advises. "Always be on the lookout for great blogs and ask if you can include them on your blogroll. It's a great way to network as well as to keep visitors interested and coming back."

Claudia's talents are many, but she would like to burnish her skills in Web design and PhotoShop. She also wishes that her blog's template wasn't so "static"— she would love to add more widgets. But overall, Claudia is perfectly content with how blogging has brought a living, breathing scrapbook into her life.

Claudia's favorite daily reads: aestheteslament.blogspot.com, enseignedegersaint.typepad.fr, espritchampetre.canalblog.com, frenchessence.blogspot.com

the paris apartment

now is the winter of contentment

Other Stuff

somethings about me

Find her: pixieblossoms.com

Blogs about: crafting, decorating, photography, sewing

On Pixie Blossoms, Zee Longnecker tells the stories of her life in beautiful color photographs. Whether she posts about decorating, something she has made, or her family, her pictures are what draw readers in. When it comes to creating your blog, Zee says, "Find your niche and stick to it. Be yourself, be unique. Personally, I like nice photos. Keeping a blog has been a good excuse to improve my photography skills."

Zee knew from the start that she wanted a unique-looking blog, so she spent time learning the basics of HTML and more advanced computer design. The results of her hard work can be seen on her amazing blog. "I have my own aesthetics and I have built the template design with my ideas, using royalty-free vintage images," she says. "It took some months to be satisfied with the current template."

Zee supports everyone in breaking through their fears and overcoming any technology challenges. "If you are going to start your own blog, learn a bit of HTML," she advises. "Knowing the basics will give you the knowledge to do things like change your banner, place links and photographs in copy, add unique-looking blogrolls on your sidebar, and so many other things."

Not always feeling creative is an issue Zee shares with most bloggers. "There are days that I just don't feel like blogging," says the Brazil native who now lives in Arizona. "I also don't write in my mother language, so I am always wondering about my English."

At the end of the day, though, she loves the learning process of blogging. "I learn a lot of things because I have a blog," Zee says. "It's fun to have something new to show my readers and see their comments. Blogging has taught me that I am creative and creativity has no limits."

Zee has some important advice for anyone thinking about starting a blog. "Remember that the Internet is open for anyone," she says. "Most of your readers will be strangers. Think about what you are going to show on your blog. Blog safely."

Zee's favorite daily reads: decor8blog.com, creature comforts.typepad.com, kidshaus.typepad.com

BEAUTY and the BLOG

Who doesn't love a little bling? By bling I don't mean blinking graphics, but other elements like fabulous wallpaper backgrounds, unique fonts, and elegant frames around images. Your blog reflects your personal taste and style. It can look fun and funky, retro, vintage, romantic, or cool and clean. Regardless of style, it can have a strong and dedicated following. Some come for the beauty, while others may come for the content. Finding your style may take you a few tries to get it right. Do what works for you. The most important thing in blissful blogging is to just be yourself. This advice is repeated time and again by the top creative bloggers interviewed for this book. Readers will pick up on your honesty and keep reading.

It's a Visual Thing

Photos can make or break a creative, blissful blog. When I polled readers on my own site, 91 percent of them said they would rather see a photo that doesn't match the post than no photo at all. What does this mean for your own site? Simply that when you post, the curtains don't have to match the couch.

I find that my posts tend to follow my photos, as it's the photo that usually inspires my post. Nothing is off limits for a photo shoot. I'll catch the kids doing something cute (snap), a bird's nest in a tree (snap), my muddy boots out on a hike (snap), or the latest finds at a flea mart (snap). When pulled together, those little snapshots make up a full day. I carry my digital SLR camera wherever I go. My blog has inspired me to look at life more artistically, to take better photos, and to focus on the little things. If my words or musing aren't directly inspired by one of my snapshots, I'll include a photo that has nothing to do with the post, making sure it's pretty and inspiring in some form.

Creative bloggers are visual people and they want to see inspiration, so be sure to give it to them. The images you use can be as simple as a photo of some ribbons in your studio, beautiful flowers in the garden, or your baby's sandy toes. Readers respond well to photographs of life's small details; they like simplicity and the beauty in everyday objects. Creating stunning and inspiring images does not have to be difficult or too involved. There's no need to go overboard. Unfussy shots are more inspiring than elaborately staged ones.

Visit your favorite blogs for inspiration for your own photographs. Make notes about the photos that you like. What makes them special? Do they feature people or nature? Are they images of overall rooms or details like a pretty pillow, hat, or craft project? What kind of angles did the photographer use? Taking the time to think these things through will help you be prepared to create your own beautiful images.

Alys Geertsen of Paris Couture Antiques customized her blog with a unique background, cool fonts, and frames.

Raised in Cotton is the name of Carol Spinski's blog. Feminine fonts, a colored background, and frames add just the right amount of bling to this beautiful blog.

Wonderful surprises are everywhere, if you just stop to look. Beauty can often be found in life's simple moments. I took these photographs while hanging out with my kids, on days we were doing just regular, ordinary things. I carry my digital SLR camera with me wherever I go so I don't miss the opportunity to record these types of images for my blog.

How to Take Great Photos

Photographer Sara Ducket of Sadie Olive Photography and the blog sadieolive.typepad.com shares her tips for creating beautiful photographs and posting them to your blog on the following pages.

Lighting

Natural light always looks best in photographs. Using a flash or indoor lamp will give your images an unnatural yellow hue, cause red eye, or will make your images dark. When at all possible wait until the sun provides natural lighting through a window or take some of your images outdoors.

Zoom

Get a little closer to your subject. Photos are much more interesting to your readers when they can make out all of the tiny details you thought made the moment worth capturing.

Focus

Did you know that your own movement is responsible for most of the blurry images you have taken? A tripod will help keep your images in focus by keeping your camera steady. There are quite a few inexpensive tripods available. If you don't want to invest in extra equipment, try resting your arms on a table top when taking a picture so that the camera is held as steady as possible. You can also stand with your feet slightly apart to help anchor your body when a tabletop or an armrest is not nearby.

Quality

Even the very best photographers will take several shots of the same subject to ensure they get a single good one. Don't be afraid to take 20–50 photos to capture a great moment. With digital photography, there is no reason to feel wasteful. Simply delete the ones you think are less than perfect.

Quantity

Be careful not to add too many photos to a single post or allow too many posts to show on a single page. Doing so will make your blog painfully slow to load for your readers with a slow Internet connection. Limit the number of posts on a single page to ten. (You can change this through the settings in your control panel.)

Sizing

Learn how to use a photo-editing program such as Microsoft Paint (standard software on most PCs) or iPhoto (standard software on most Macintosh computers) to properly size your photos. Images taken straight from the camera are usually very large files and need to be resized before posting online. You will want to keep the proportions of your image intact when resizing or your photo will get distorted. Images may be resized smaller without hurting the quality of the image, but making an image larger will lessen the quality. It is a good idea to save the original large camera files in one folder, and the resized smaller images in another folder, so that you have both copies.

Make it easy on your readers by giving your images center stage. Avoid using the smallest image settings in your posts, and opt for the largest images your blog will allow. Most blogs will accommodate pictures up to 400 pixels wide in your blog posts. (Some allow even larger images.) Play with these settings until you find the size that best fits your blog. The image itself should be at least as large as the size you choose or it will get distorted; this means that if you want your image to be 400 pixels by 350 pixels in your blog, you need to save the image at that size.

Protection

Protect your work from copyright infringement. Use a photo-editing program to put your name in the images you post. Simple select the Type tool, choose white as the color and type on the image. This will deter

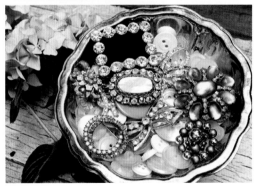

If you are overwhelmed by everything in a room, choose one detail to feature and take a close-up picture of it. These kinds of vignettes can be found all around you. Notice how the chandelier sparkles when it is the center of attention, or how the colors of the books draw you in, or how exquisite the vintage baubles look when they are all displayed together.

Framing your photos means more than adding something around the edges. It also refers to the area you choose to feature in your photograph. When looking through the viewfinder, be thoughtful of the area around and behind the subject of your photo. You may wish to show more of a beautiful background or focus tightly on a flower or other element in the frame.

people from trying to use your images elsewhere. This does not fully protect your images as they can be cropped or manipulated to remove the text. However, there are software programs that can embed your copyright directly into the image and prevent any cropping or image manipulation.

Embellishments

As you get more comfortable editing photos, consider using digital scrapbooking frames and details to adorn your blog and photos. This will not only give your images a fresh new look, but there are endless possibilities for design.

Frame Your Photos

One look I absolutely love to see on blogs is the use of frames around images. Frames enhance images and tie visual elements together. Once you are comfortable taking great images and including them in your posts, adding frames to your images isn't difficult. Each blog host offers options for adding frames to images; visit your blog's home page or dashboard for how-to information. Another option is to use digital frames. Digital frames can be downloaded from various websites. To find sites that offer them, do a search for "digital frames" or "digital scrapbooking."

In order to add frames to your images, you will need a photo-editing program such as PhotoShop Elements, a software program geared for use by non-professionals. It also costs about one-third the price of the full version of PhotoShop. If you want to enhance digital images on a regular basis, PhotoShop Elements and similar programs should be in your digital arsenal.

Using Digital Frames

On her website, cottagearts.net, designer and artist Michelle Shefveland provides digital scrapbooking and photography ideas and digital products and tutorials to help creative types make the most of their digital images and art. Here she shows how to add digital frames to images for use on creative blogs.

Instructions

The instructions here were written for Adobe PhotoShop Elements 7 (PSE 7). However, Adobe PhotoShop CS+ and other versions of PhotoShop Elements, and Corel Paint Shop Pro are almost identical. Michelle has made free digital frames available on her website for use with this tutorial. Digital scrapbooking sites will also offer many options.

1. Download free CottageArtsScrapEdgeSampler.zip file from www.cottagearts.net/samples.html. Unzip.

2. Open PhotoShop Elements.

3. Choose File > Open and browse to find the Scrap.Edge.jpg file. Click Open. (On the left is what it looks like as an unfinished graphic file.)

4. Repeat Step 3 to open desired photo (shown above right). Drag the Scrap.Edge on top of the photo image.

5. Move and re-size the Scrap.Edge to fit the size of the photo using the Move Tool. Note that this sample Scrap.Edge is in 6" x 6" proportions at 300 dpi, but will still look pretty good at other aspect ratios.

6. Now we are going to take it one step further and fill the Scrap.Edge with another color that's more complementary to the photo and then play with the Layer Blend Modes to add some unique color effects.

The images above have all been embellished with digital frames. I keep a few framing options in my digital arsenal because each one lends a different look and feel to images. I love the scrapbook feel to the image of me and my father. Notice how using the same frame around the images at the bottom pulls them all together.

Before

After

The before and after images that accompany the framing tutorial are beautiful examples of how digital frames enhance and can even change the mood of images. Michelle Shefveland used the same method as the tutorial, just with different frames, to produce the results on these pages. Her before images are all wonderful in their own right, but the after examples are spectacular.

Step 8

7. Select the Foreground color chip on the tool bar and sample a desired color from the photo. Here is a sample dark green from the background, color #141808 (above).

8. In the layer palette, Ctrl-Click (Mac: Option-Click) with the mouse on the Scrap.Edge to Select the shape.

9. Select Edit > Fill and choose Foreground Color in the Fill Dialog box. Click OK to fill the Scrap.Edge with this color.

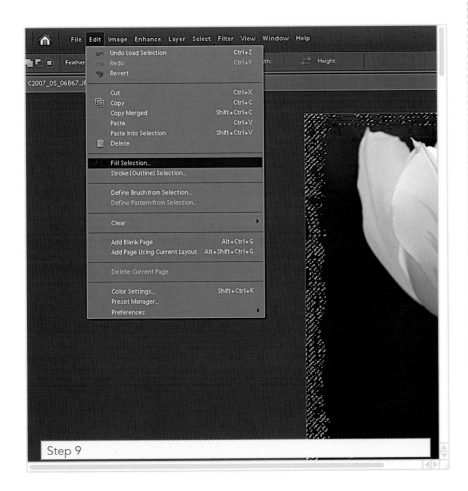

Step 9

Before

After

Before

After

10. An optional step is to add a texture paper overlay, creating a more textured image (so very popular in photography right now). Repeat Step 3 to open desired paper for blending. Look for one with great texture or paint strokes. (Shown here: #10 in CottageArts' Naturals 13 Paper Pak.) Drag this paper onto the photo.

11. Now, for the fun part! Play with the Layer Blend Modes on all of the layers in the layer palette. Shown here is the Overlay for the textured paper layer and Soft Light for the Scrap.Edge.

Before

After

Step 12

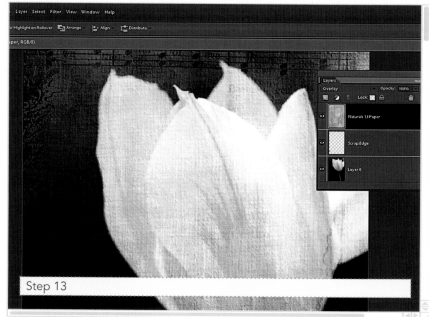

Step 13

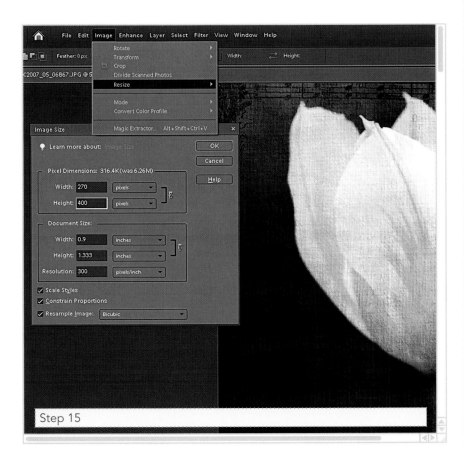

Step 15

Before

After

12. Experiment with the opacity of the layers, as you can be so creative in this step.

13. Save as a .psd file to retain layers, if you want to edit again.

14. For your blog, re-size the image to 400 pixels (Image>Resize) wide or high (longest side). Select File > Save for Web and in dialog box, select medium quality JPEG. Click OK.

Image is now ready to post to your blog!

After years of fancy frills (left), I have decided to go with a cleaner look for my blog (right).

From Blah to Aah

One way to jazz up your blog is to use fancy sidebar decorations when adding things, such as the "About" link, to your blog's sidebar. You can create the elements yourself or have a designer do it for you.

For my own blog, I decided to take down my fancy sidebar decorations and just be me. I'm not a plain Jane by any means, but I like things simple, casual, and elegant, whether it's my home, my clothes, or my blog. After making this change, readership doubled and I was getting thousands of hits a day from all over the world.

Building a Banner

Oh how we love banners! For many bloggers, their banner is like their front door at home. It says, "Come on in, have a cup a coffee, and let's catch up." Banners should reflect your personal style and help set the tone of your blog. Change banners frequently to keep your blog looking fresh and exciting. I change my banner with the seasons or whenever the mood strikes. Changing your banner can bring visitors back to see what you are up to next. I am always looking for seasonal ideas and inspiration. It's also fun to see what is inspiring to other creative bloggers.

One style of banner is the graphic banner. Created using graphics or other layered elements, including photographs, this banner style is used to help brand an image, or by bloggers who just love the look.

Another type of banner is a photo banner. My banner is nothing fancy, just a personal photo that has been resized. A lovely shot of pumpkins on your front steps in the fall, a shot of toes in the sand in the summer, or even a shot of favorite things in your studio can be a wonderful way to welcome visitors to your blog.

The simplest banner consists of your blog's name in text. This is the easiest banner to create because no graphics or images are used. Every blog host offers text-style banners as part of their most basic templates.

Teri and Serena, the women behind The Farm Chicks, use tag graphics to hold their sidebar titles. Retro-looking embellishments enhance the theme of their blog.

Custom elements like the sidebar fancies seen on the French Garden House can take a blog from boring to beautiful.

Consider taking yourself on photography dates. All you need is your camera. Head outdoors or walk around the house to find interesting subjects. Practice framing your images in different ways: pull in tight, or show more background, and work with the settings on your camera to vary the lighting. The more you practice, the better your results will be.

The Right Fit

Though some blog host services will automatically resize images to use on a blog, many do not. Images are such an important element of creative blogs, so resizing them is one very necessary skill.

To ready images for use on your blog, you will need to use a photo-editing program. Macintosh computers have a standard program called iPhoto, and PCs have a standard program called Microsoft Paint. The full version of PhotoShop is for the computer-savvy and technical user, while PhotoShop Elements is for the beginner.

Full-scale photo-editing software programs, such as Adobe Photo-Shop, will allow you to resize images, manipulate color, and much more. Here is how to resize images with the standard programs on Macs and PCs.

Resizing a photo using iPhoto

1. Open image in iPhoto.

2. Click on File in the tool bar. From the drop-down menu, click Export, then click on the Kind and Size options. The Kind option has five file formats to choose from. Three of these allow you to resize the image: JPEG, PNG, or TIFF. Choose JPEG.

3. In the Size option, select Custom. Select the desired height and width.

4. Click Export and then save the image to a location on your computer.

Resizing a photo using Microsoft Paint

1. To open Microsoft Paint, click Start, Programs, Accessories, and then Paint.

2. Open the image file you wish to edit.

3. Click the Image menu located in the tool bar and select Stretch/ Skew Image.

4. Choose a percentage figure to resize the image. To avoid distortion, choose the same percentage for horizontal and vertical stretch.

5. Click OK to view resized image on screen. To check image size, click Image, Attributes, and then choose pixels to see the exact size of the image. Repeat steps 1 to 5 until your image is the desired size.

6. When you are finished resizing the image, click File, then Save As and save the image with a new file name. Using the Save As option will prevent you from overwriting the original image.

Working with photo-editing software

In addition to resizing images, full-service photo-editing software programs allow you to add text to an image. This feature comes in handy, especially when creating a photo banner. Catherine of Avalon Rose Designs created the following tutorial in PhotoShop to help you create a photo banner, resize photos, and add text to images with ease.

Creating a photo banner

Creating a banner for your blog from a photo is very easy, and involves only a few steps. It's pretty much a combination of cropping, resizing, and adding text.

The first thing you need to do is find a suitable photo. You need to be aware of copyright law when choosing a photo. You own the copyright to any photo that you have personally taken; however, if the photo that you have taken includes people, you may need to get a model release to publish the photo online. The same goes for photos that have products or items with logos displayed. Using someone else's logo can get you in trouble.

If you are looking online for photos, you can't just go to Google images and pick one off the Internet. Most of those images are copyright protected. Think about it this way—you most likely wouldn't want others

These images have all been cropped or enhanced with photo-editing software. The colors of the shells were brightened and the crop on the yarn was tightened.

When viewed in full, this image is boring. Also, the ballerina is so small, it seems like she really wasn't supposed to be there.

Once the image is cropped, however, the ballerina seems animated and she adds a playful, artistic element to the image.

taking your photos and using them, so don't do it to someone else. To be on the safe side, you need to look for public domain photos. There are several resources for public domain images/photos, including one that has more than 5,000 public domain images. The name of the site is public-domain-photos.com. Keep in mind, though, that the best way to create unique posts that keep readers coming back for more is to use unique content—in the end it may be best to take your own images.

Cropping photographs

Since PhotoShop has the awesome ability to crop and resize an image in one step, this won't take long. Most photos downloaded directly from your digital camera are too large to use on the Web. You need to know the width you will need for your banner (also known as a photo header). This is going to depend on the width of your blog layout,

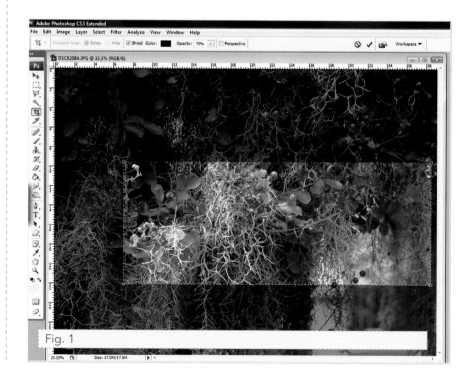

Fig. 1

most of which are set at 800 pixels wide or smaller. Some blogs will automatically resize your header when you upload it so that it will fit in the space allowed. As for height, that is going to be a personal preference, although I recommend going absolutely no taller than 300 pixels. For the example in this tutorial, I'm going to create a photo blog header of 750 pixels wide by 300 pixels tall.

Though all of the elements in this image are pretty, the overall effect is a bit cold. It feels like you walked into the frame before things were finished.

Fig. 2

Cropping tight into the image results in a lovely, warm, and inviting vignette.

After you find the perfect photo, open it in PhotoShop and follow the instructions for cropping to a specific size. Use 750 px in the width box and 300 px in the height box (Fig. 1). If your photo is large enough, you can be picky about what part of the photo you want to be in the header. Once you have it where you want it, click the checkmark located at the top of the screen. Your image will be cropped (Fig 2).

If once you've cropped the image, you don't like it, go to the toolbar, click Edit >Step Backward, and try it again. Next you will need to add text, and you can follow the tutorial for adding text to images for that. When dealing with a blog header, you may want a fun, unique, or funky font. There are so many places to download fonts online.

This pretty image is of my niece and nephew. My niece was so patient as I took this picture! In this version, her dress and shoes are a bit distracting.

The intimate feel seen here was easily achieved by eliminating the distracting elements with a tighter crop.

Fig. 3

My favorite commercial font sites are myfonts.com and fontbros.com, both of which have a fantastic selection. Free font sites can be a little tricky, because some have those really annoying pop-ups; you have to be careful about what you are downloading to your computer. Two free font sites that I've used are dafont.com and abstractfonts.com.

Fig. 4

Just keep in mind when you're choosing a font that people need to be able to read it. There are many fonts out there that are really cool, but when added to a photo, can be hard to read.

Choosing your text color is important, too. If your photo has a dark section, add light-colored text there or vice versa. If your photo's coloration widely varies like my example photo, you may want to consider other options like adding a drop shadow to your text, as in the example on the top left of page 88 (Fig. 3). Think about the placement of your text as well. Your text does not have to be centered directly in the middle of your header.

If your text is still difficult to read, you may consider adding a translucent shape behind your text (Fig. 4). You will need to use the Shape tool, and you can activate that by hitting the U key on your keyboard. Set your foreground color to white and draw a rectangle behind your text. Then, in your Layers window, be sure the shape layer you just drew is behind the text layer. Then adjust the opacity of the shape layer so that while your photo shows through, the text is more legible.

Type A, B & C Personalities

In fashion you can't go wrong with black, but on a blog it's not the same equation. Colors and fonts set the entire mood for your blog, so consider your audience when choosing what you will use. Are you a modern crafty blogger who loves clean, bright graphics? Then clear, bright colors could be wonderful accents on your blog. Do you love all things vintage? Then a more muted color palette may be just what is needed. When choosing a background color for your blog, remember that it is much easier to read dark text on a light background than light text on a dark background. When in doubt, go white; it's always in style.

This romantic room is pretty, but it's difficult to make out any of the details.

Focusing in on the feminine tabletop makes for a more attractive image and gives the eye something to rest on.

missyballance.typepad.com

Missy Ballance uses colored type on her blog, Crafty Carnival. It works well because she uses complementary colors that are easy on the eyes.

To add visual interest, Jenny Harris uses a variety of fonts on her blog.

Sometimes fonts can be a nuisance to readers. Always go for an easy-to-read font for your posts, such as Tahoma, Times New Roman, or Verdana (all are standard on any blog platform). A nice size would be 9 or 10 point. Most blog hosts have a limited set of fonts you can use for your blog posts and they are all Web-safe fonts that can be viewed on all types of browsers. Just because you can see a certain fancy font on your screen doesn't mean everyone else can.

Because banners and sidebar elements are saved as images and not body copy, feel free to use more unusual or pretty fonts on the sidebar or banner elements. There are several websites that offer fabulous fonts. Veer.com and Myfonts.com have a huge selection of unique and stylish fonts, but they come with a price tag and charge per font.

Casual Fonts (I use these for posting.)	*Dressy & Scripty Fonts* (I use these on my banners.)
Arial	Brock Script
Helvetica	Cezanne
Tahoma	Edwardian
Times New Roman	Hurricane
Trebuchet	Mahogany Script
Verdana	Passion Conflict

Modern Fonts	*Playful & Thematic Fonts*
Century Gothic	HERCULANUM
ECCENTRIC STD	Marker Felt
Futura	Party LET
Helvetica Neue (Light)	PRINCETOWN

For free fonts that are just as pretty, try Urbanfonts.com. Or, just do a search for fonts and find the ones you love. Most fontware sites have instructions for downloading, but always be sure to download the fonts into the font library on your hard drive.

Adding Custom Banners and Sidebar Fancies

Two custom elements that can make a huge impact on the look of your blog are your banner and sidebar fancies. Here, designer and blogger Sara Duckett provides tutorials on adding them to your blog. Sara creates blog designs for use on Blogger and TypePad. For WordPress you can find countless places for help online.

Adding a custom banner

The first step is to make sure your banner is the correct size before uploading it to your blog. To ready your banner or sidebar elements for uploading to your blog, files will need to be saved as image files. The most common type is a JPEG or .jpg, though .gif files also can be used. The size will depend on the settings you are using for your blog, but a basic rule of thumb is that a two-column blog will take a banner width of around 660 pixels across. A three-column blog will take a banner width of 770 pixels across. A three-column blog on TypePad with a center column that is 500 pixels-wide will take an 870 pixels-wide banner. The height doesn't matter as much but typical height would be around 300 to 350 pixels. (The height will determine how far down someone has to scroll to see the content on your blog. If your banner is too tall, they may only see the banner on the page and nothing else unless they scroll down.)

To add the banner to Blogger, log onto your control panel, choose "edit" next to the blog header box at the top of your layout page, and then upload your resized banner. If your banner already includes text in the image, then choose "instead of blog name and description." Then click save.

TypePad provides answers to creating various types of custom banners in their knowledge base.

My custom banners always consist of an image and my blog name. I use images because I can easily change them out whenever I choose.

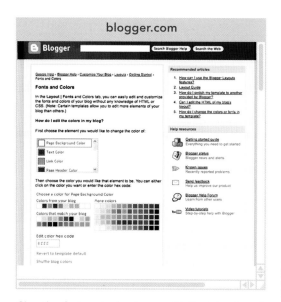

Changing fonts and colors is easy with the help of tutorials like this one from Blogger.com.

Heather Bullard created this amazing collage for her blog, Vintage Living, at flickr.com.

To add a banner to TypePad, log into your control panel, and click on the name of your blog. Choose the "design" tab from the blue tabs across the top. Click on "theme." Click on "Text or Image" under the word "Banner" at the top of the screen. This will reveal another menu; choose "image" then upload your resized banner. Scroll down to click "Save Changes."

Adding sidebar fancies

Sidebar fancies can be a great way to personalize the look of your blog and give it a bit of personality. To begin, you will need to save the image or graphic element as a GIF file to your computer. Remember where you save it so that you can find it again.

To add sidebar fancies using Blogger, go to your control panel, click on the "layout" page. Click "add an item" to your sidebar. Choose "image" as the type. Upload the GIF file you saved to your computer. Click save.

To add sidebar fancies using TypePad, go to your control panel. Click on the green control panel tab at the top of the screen. Then select "files" from the blue tabs. Upload the GIF file you saved to your computer. Pay close attention to the name of the file. In this example we will name the file "blinkie.gif." Then click "Typelists" from the green tabs across the top.

Click "Create a new Typelist." Select "notes" as the list type. Name the list whatever you want to show on your blog, for example, "As seen On." Click "create new list." In the blank box entitled "notes" you must then write the HTML code to get the image you uploaded to display. It should look something like this: <img src = http://the-nameofyourblog.typepad.com/my_weblog/blinkie.gif >. Make sure you have your blog address correct and the file name correct. Click "save." Click on the blue "publish" tab at the top. Select the box next to your blog and hit "save changes."

Sources for Art and Visuals

There are places to go on the Web for beautiful imagery if you don't have your own yet (try to experiment with your own camera; you may be surprised at your ability to capture something pretty). If you are in a hurry, stop by these places for some great stock photos that charge a nominal fee for images: Getty Images (gettyimages.com/creative) and iStockphoto.com. Flickr.com is also a great source for beautiful photos—and they're free. However, you must get permission from the owner. Blissful bloggers can also host their own photos at Flickr for free as well. Flickr is an online photo management site that lets you upload and share images and more. For extra blog beauty you can even link to your Flickr site directly from your blog. Photobucket.com is another online photo management website you can use.

What You Can and Can't Use

This is a hot topic on blogs. You wouldn't just go into your neighbor's yard and cut flowers from their blooming garden. You'd ask permission, right? The same rules apply in blogdom. Most blogs post a copyright notice in their sidebar that states something like, "Photos are copyrighted, please do not use without my written permission." And they mean it! Most bloggers are happy to share, just send an email asking to use the photo, wait for that written permission, and always give credit to the blogger with a link back to their blog.

Here is an example of how to approach a blogger to use a photo: "Hi, my name is Kelly Ann, and I am posting today about my ribbon collection. I would love to use your photo in my post to inspire others, and will include a link to your blog. I will await your response and thank you for your time." After approval, you will need to credit the owner of the photo in your blog post by writing something like: "Photo above courtesy of so and so from suchandsuch.typepad.com."

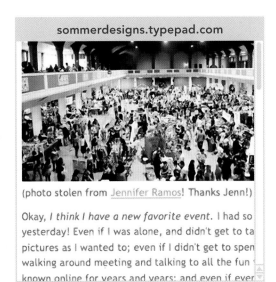

Carrie Sommers credited another photographer for the image from an event they both attended.

Heather Bailey's copyright disclaimer is friendly and easy to read. To protect your images and text, you should always include a copyright disclaimer such as this on your blog.

Find her: sadieolive.typepad.com
Blogs about: business, design, home décor, photography

Sara Duckett may just have one blog, but her artistic presence is felt in many, many ways. This talented designer, who hails from Tustin, California, has made a name for herself helping other like-minded bloggers design spectacular banners and home pages.

Sara began to blog a few years ago as a way for her customers to get to know her better (her website, sadieolive.com, offers a tempting array of chic French and vintage items). Now, with business going so well, Sara considers her blog as more of a personal expression. "It's about lifestyle, décor ideas, photos that inspire me, and just everyday stuff," she says.

The name Sadie Olive, picked out by Sara and her husband for the daughter they've yet to have, has been cherished by them through years of infertility battles. "I decided to put the name we chose to good use as the name of my business," Sara explains. She is very happy with the choice and wouldn't have it any other way.

Her biggest challenge is finding enough interesting stories to relate (although you'd never be able to tell). More often than not, a single photograph she's taken will give her the inspiration she needs to write.

Sara also finds herself getting "lost in blogland" instead of working. Still, she tries very hard to leave comments wherever she roams. "Blog owners love to get comments," she says. "Do take the time to leave messages and visit other blogs so that yours will be visited in return." Consider it your public relations and marketing hour (or two).

Sara's great eye for the one-of-a-kind mixed with her cutting-edge talents with photography and Photo-Shop are the perfect partners for a life of blogging.

Sara's favorite daily reads: cathypentondesigns.blogspot.com, heatherbullard.typepad.com, lolabboutique.blogspot.com, raisedincotton.typepad.com, teresaksheeley.typepad.com

Le Journal   About Me   Sadie Olive Design   Boutique   Photography   Design Portfolio   Shades of Inspiration   In the Press   Archives
Subscribe

HEATHER BULLARD: Vintage Inspired Living

Find her: heatherbullard.typepad.com
Blogs about: business, design, photography

Sometimes, our means to an end becomes the end itself. This happened to Heather Bullard, who in 2006 started her blog as just a way to learn more about building a website. In the end, Vintage Inspired Living brought Heather lots of loyal readers and great exposure for her talents as a photographer and stylist. It now serves as a beautiful entryway to her online shop, thepresentpast.com.

"I never kept a journal and now I finally have one," says Heather, who tries to focus on capturing the beauty in simple, everyday pursuits—family celebrations, a must-visit shop, a great book, and her ongoing flea market adventures. "Inspiration is all around you if you take the time to notice," she says.

Heather is known for the amazing photographs she takes as well as the exquisite vintage jewelry, ephemera, and decorative accessories she sells on her website. Besides regular blogging and running her virtual shop,

Heather also stays busy contributing to many magazines. Sometimes it's difficult to do it all and spend time with her family, so Heather doesn't fret if she misses a day or two of posting. When she does post, she pays careful attention to the details—the heading, for example. Headers are very important for luring readers who tend to skim (pretty much everyone).

She also has some great advice on taking photographs: "Try to post large, clear photos, especially closeups."

We can all learn much from the talented Ms. Bullard. She advises us not to clutter our blogs with too many items in the sidebars, and to learn how to use our blogging format so we can change our own banner and update our own blogs.

Heather's favorite daily reads: blomsterverkstad. blogspot.com, rebeccasower.typepad.com, theinspired room.net

Find her: inkvanilla.typepad.com
Blogs about: art, everyday life, journaling

As her finger paused over the "Publish" button that fateful day two years ago, June Parrish Cookson felt apprehension sending out her first post to the world. She did it, however, and the world is definitely a better place with Ink Vanilla in it.

Her blog's name comes from June's unique artistry, which combines illustrative art and whimsical prose on vanilla-tone paper.

Ink Vanilla is purely about bliss. June's need to reach out and commune with other artists has been deeply satisfied through her blog. "My intent (with blogging) was and still remains to express myself through art and prose," she explains. "It is a fascinating and fulfilling journey interacting with, and being inspired by, fellow artists."

Learning the ropes and acquiring the confidence in the beginning was tough, June says. She suggests that beginning bloggers nourish their site as if it were a newborn. Give it lots of attention and be patient as it grows and changes. There will be days when you don't feel quite as inspired, or even very happy about life. June admits that there are times when her own lack of enthusiasm resulted in dismal feedback from readers. But each new day brings a fresh perspective, and June's readers delight in the way she captures the beauty of ordinary pursuits.

June is often surprised at how deeply readers reach to find months-old posts about her moleskine journals, or to ask her if they can use her masquerade game at their next party. Some illustration assignments and other paid projects have come out of it as well.

June's biggest pet peeve is people using someone else's photos without asking permission. She takes blogging very seriously and feels that everyone should treat blogging with the utmost respect.

"Blogging has expanded my mind and heart to be more inspired by the little things, things I would never have taken notice of in the past," she says. "It has developed an awareness that brings new challenges and produces more layers of experience."

June's favorite daily reads: euroantiquemarket. blogspot.com, poppytalk.blogspot.com, sfgirlbybay. blogspot.com

LIDY BAARS: Little French Garden House

Find her: littlefrenchgardenhouse.blogspot.com
Blogs about: antiques, business, family, flea markets

Lidy Baars has never met a flea market she didn't like; or an antique shop either, for that matter. This talented designer from California says her blog, Little French Garden House, is a "pastiche," or in plain English, a little bit of everything. She writes about the antiques world and her visits to flea markets. She shares the ups and downs of being an entrepreneur, a woman in business, and her European heritage. But one of her favorite subjects to write about is her European gardener, who happens to be her husband.

Lidy's blog entries are inspired by her life and business. When she makes a discovery, she lets the history of the piece and her imagination do the talking. "All things old have a story to tell," Lidy says. "I love to wonder who might have owned a painting or old tiara I picked up at a market, and so I blog about it."

Readers respond to the beauty on Little French Garden House. Whether it's a single rose, an antique perfume bottle, or a table setting, the images remind us that we flourish when we are able to respond to beauty in our world and when we can create our own.

Lidy says her blog, where she has a sidebar link to her boutique, has been the most powerful marketing tool for her Internet business. She mixes what's new in the shop with her everyday life and is able to show photos of her favorite merchandise.

Her advice to new bloggers: Don't be afraid to start. Set up your blog and add frills and a pretty header later.

"It doesn't have to be perfect right away," she says. Visit other blogs, leave meaningful comments, and soon, she says, you'll know you're a diehard blogger because you: 1) Carry your camera everywhere; and 2) Mutter under your breath, "Oh, this is a perfect shot for my blog."

Lidy's favorite daily reads: donnaobrien.type pad. com, storybookwoods.typepad.com, the-feathered-nest. blogspot.com

Antiques and Shabby Decor to Romance your Home & Garden

ANDREA SINGARELLA: Everyday Beauty

Find her: velvetstrawberries.typepad.com
Blogs about: crafting, decorating, gift-giving, shopping

After months of fence-sitting, wondering if she should take the leap, Andrea Singarella jumped into blog writing in 2007 and has never looked back. Everyday Beauty is a photographic documentation of the pretty little details of Andrea's life that she finds inspiring and that bring her joy. She often blogs about topics such as decorating, and what she calls "nesting"—crafting, shopping flea markets for vintage treasures, the art of gift-giving, baking, and special celebrations.

"Blogging is the perfect outlet for sharing snippets of my passions and creative style with other like-minded women," Andrea says. "We're all striving to incorporate beauty in the details of everyday life."

Andrea believes every blog is unique because each author puts her own fingerprint on every picture and every word that is typed. She tries to write like she speaks in real life, in a down-to-earth, conversational tone, creating a real-life diary with inspiring glimpses into her world. Her world is a happy, light-hearted, and pretty place on the Web.

When there are stresses in her life, Andrea says it can be challenging to not let them show up on her blog. So she tries to avoid that by focusing on positive topics that inspire both her and her readers. This conscious choice can be quite therapeutic. "My blog has taught me to slow down and take time to enjoy the little things in my life," Andrea says.

Simple pleasures are abundant and one only needs to take the time to notice them to enjoy their Everyday Beauty.

Andrea's favorite daily reads: "Any blog with lots of pictures and frequent posts."

KARI RAMSTROM: Artsy Mama

Find her: artsymama.blogspot.com
Blogs about: art, business, family life, swaps

One cold autumn day in Plymouth, Minnesota, Kari Ramstrom started a blog. An avid journaler while growing up, Kari saw that blogging was the next logical step in her creative outreach. "I wanted something I could share with the world," Kari says. "I also wanted to hold myself accountable, to make blogging a habit."

This was no small feat for this busy artist, thrifter, writer, and photographer, but Kari had a strong vision—to create "trails of inspiration" that meander through family life, her art, and her business, offering one beautiful collection. She also immediately understood the importance of building community with her blog. She draws huge crowds when she posts about an art event like Junk Bonanza. One of her other big draws is the swaps she hosts.

Swaps are like virtual gift exchanges; guests sign up and are paired with another guest. After getting to know each other a bit, the two exchange gifts based on the swap's theme. "Afterward, we post our treasures on Flickr," Kari says. "So many guests have made really close friends as a result of participating in a swap."

Building community in innovative ways, marketing her Etsy shop, and writing her self-published book has paid off for Kari. "I've exceeded what I thought my blog would bring me tenfold over the last three years," she says. "I have been given numerous opportunities that I would never have had if I didn't have a blog."

One thing Kari wishes is that she knew more about the technical side of blog design. "I'd like to change the look of my blog more frequently but have to rely on the tech savvy of friends," she admits. But blogging has become an important part of her life, and she has come to rely on the like-minded community blogging has brought her.

Kari's favorite daily reads: aliedwards.typepad.com, kerismith.com/blog

Find her: loobylu.com

Blogs about: books, creative ideas and projects, family, inspiration, life, work

Claire Robinson began her blog, Loobylu, in December 1999 and has been part of blogdom from the beginning. "I was working in a very small Internet start-up and I discovered the then-tiny world of online journaling and it looked like a lot of fun," says the Australian native. "Having always kept a diary, it seemed like an easy choice."

This incredibly popular blogger says she didn't have any particular expectations from her blog when she started. "It was a bit of a brave new world back then," says Claire. "I was excited (immensely) when I discovered I had a reader apart from my husband."

Blogging has always offered Claire a unique sense of freedom. "When I first started the blog, it was mostly just a form of creative expression," she says. "My work was designing websites for clients, and I quite often found it frustrating and far from creative. I was keen to create something that was just for me—something I could play around with and control the look of and the content just seemed to follow."

Of her blog's unique name, Claire says, "I was looking for a name to blog under anonymously, and I ended up going through some children's rhymes for inspiration. 'Here we go loobylu, here we go loobyli' just seemed right." Claire likes the freedom of blogging, the fact that you can change your blog whenever you want. "The beauty of blogging is that you can try things and then let them go if they don't work," she says. "You're not really hemmed into something. If you start off writing about craft, then you can easily transition into writing about family or travel, so there are rarely any regrets."

If growing an audience matters to you, Claire advises that you update regularly—at least three times a week, if not more. If writing is not your strength, she suggests that you find time to take good photos and learn how to use simple photo-editing programs to improve them. "Don't expect to have a big audience immediately," she says. "It takes time and patience to grow an audience, especially now that there are bazillions of blogs. In the end, a blog that brings you pleasure will bring pleasure to others."

Claire's favorite daily reads: soulemama.com, angry chicken.typepad.com, meetmeatmikes.com, weewon derfuls.typepad.com, dancingwithfrogs.com

Loobylu

Home   About   Contact

Writing in the new year

Subscribe to Loobylu!

Ads by Google A V

September Links

Free Crafting
Magazine
Crafts, scrapbooking
& keepsakes. Get

CHARLOTTE LYONS: House Wren Studio

Find her: housewrenstudio.typepad.com
Blogs about: artwork, crafts, family stories

Artist, author, and designer Charlotte Lyons has been a creative force for many years. She came to blogging as a way to connect with people involved with crafting and art. "When I started blogging, I wanted to increase my presence in the craft and design scene, get back into a world I felt was passing me by," she says. "I knew I had to make a bigger effort and learn blogging as a contemporary media trend."

Her audience quickly found her and has been loyal ever since. "The comments and support came in right away from people who had my books and new readers also," she says. "I was invited to teach and encouraged to publish again. The direct sales opportunities through blogging and Etsy are also a nice discovery."

A feathered friend inspired Charlotte to name her blog House Wren Studio. "For a number of years, a little house wren nested in the birdhouse outside my studio window," says Charlotte. "She was very busy, stayed close to home, and had the most beautiful song and chatter. I started to feel this kinship with her and came to think of her as my creative muse. My studio feels about as crowded as her birdhouse and I spend most of my day inside it." Though she does still love the name of her blog, Charlotte regrets not using her name for its name. "Later I realized that charlottelyons. typepad.com would have allowed an easier search and a flexibility for change, growth, expansion," she says.

Blogging has forced Charlotte to dig deeper into her creative well, and has yielded some wonderful benefits. "Personally, blogging has put me in touch with like-minded women and colleagues all over the world," she says. "It has also provided a way to impact the greater world through fund-raising, awareness, dialogue."

By sharing her thoughts and talents, Charlotte has reached a whole new audience, but has also experienced some difficulties. "The theft of ideas, designs, images, and words is hard," she says. "The risk in sharing so much with so many has a downside, especially for creative people who support themselves through their work."

The rewards, however, far outweigh the risks. "More than anything, I have a real community here, both professionally and personally," says Charlotte. "I love my blog friends. They inspire me, enrich me, comfort me, support me, challenge me. It has been life-changing."

Charlotte's favorite daily reads: rosylittlethings. typepad.com, soulemama.typepad.com, teresamc fayden.typepad.com, rebeccasower.typepad.com

JAMIE FINGAL: Twisted Sister

Find her: jamiefingaldesigns.blogspot.com
Blogs about: art, quilting

Jamie Fingal's mixed-media art quilts, filled with color and texture, are treasured the world over. She started her blog, Twisted Sister, as a way to show her art, and to keep family and friends updated on what she is doing.

A visit to Jamie's blog will take you on a colorful journey, full of visual eye candy and inspiration. "I wanted to be able to document my work as an artist," she says. "My blog is a way to show the public, potential clients, friends and family my up-to-date work, pieces in progress, and brief text about my journey as an artist."

Because her blog focuses on her art and business, Jamie includes links to her book, "Embellished Mini Quilts," as well as other publications and shows in which her work appears. Her extensive blogroll features artists and quilters from around the globe.

Blogging keeps Jamie working, in more ways than one. "I believe it has helped me to stay on my path as an artist, so I keep creating new and different pieces of art," she says. "Having a blog pushes me to make my best work, display the work that I am proud of, to take a risk to say that I am here." She calls her blog an interactive resume. Says Jamie, "It gives me and my art validity, and shows a potential client that they are dealing with someone who is professional, and perhaps someone they can work with."

Jamie uses her blog as a kind of virtual office. "I think that blogging is a tremendous way to communicate on so many levels," Jamie says. "I have curated quilt shows, taken pictures of the entire exhibit, and posted them on a blog for the artists to view if they could not attend the opening."

Spreading the word about her blog is something Jamie takes seriously, and she recommends other bloggers—especially those with a creative business—to do the same. "Be sure to put your URL in the signature line of every e-mail you send out," she says. "Put it on your Facebook page too, if you have one."

There is no mystery to blogging. Jamie explains, "Decide on what you want to convey, and create your blog," she advises. "Just do it; take a risk. Set up your blog, create a post, and join a Web ring for more exposure."

Jamie's favorite daily reads: aquamoonartquilts.blogspot.com, judyperez.blogspot.com, janedavila.blogspot.com, quiltingartsblog.com, studio78notes.blogspot.com

NICKY FRASER: The Vintage Magpie

Find her: thevintagemagpie.typepad.com

Blogs about: antiquing, crafting, family, friends, knitting, sewing

Nicola Fraser (known as Nicky) has been involved with crafting in one form or another her entire life. "I remember my mother was always knitting something when she had any spare time, and the comfort I felt just sitting with her while she did so is something I will never forget," says the UK-based crafter. "Now that she is no longer with me I gain a connection with her through my knitting."

Not long after she found the world of creative blogs, Nicky longed to start one of her own. "I wanted to connect with other crafters out there, and become part of this wonderful community I was discovering," she says. "I also wanted to have a way of documenting our life and precious moments." Nicky has crafted her online journal to reflect those wishes. "It's a diary of the best parts of my family life, our lifestyle and beliefs, and our beautiful surroundings. My blog serves as a wonderful account of our family memories and I love being able to revisit some old posts, and gaze at the pictures that rekindle that memory. It's also a wonderful outlet for my creativity," she says.

Her blog's name, The Vintage Magpie, reflects the content of Nicky's blog. She says, "I spent quite a long time coming up with the name. I had several ideas but The Vintage Magpie just felt right. I spend my life looking at, searching out, and desperately wanting anything that's beautiful, old and sparkling." And true to her wishes, her blog posts are filled with beautiful, heart-warming images and stories of creating and good times.

Nicky's delightful handmade mohair rabbits and bears, bags, cushions, vintage china, and ephemera are sprinkled on the pages, and bring to mind a kinder, gentler time. Her posts about family and friends make you wish you could join in the fun, and in a way, you do. "I combine my craft with an invitation for my readers to step into my lifestyle, through written and pictorial descriptions of family days out around the Devon countryside," she says. "It's an insight into my family, our lifestyle and my love of crafting, my love of anything vintage, my obsessional thrifting, and a good spoonful of old-fashioned domesticity."

Having a blog gave Nicky the confidence to develop her business and build her website. "My blog has changed my life," she says. "I now have a growing business, which allows me to work from home whilst my children are at school, and is leading me in all kinds of wonderful directions, and gives me an ever expanding circle of friends."

Nicky's favorite daily reads: lilupix.typepad.com, posy.typepad.com, nostalgiaatthestonehouse.blogspot. com, infocowboysandcustard.blogspot.com

Chapter 5

TRAFFIC
SCHOOL

So you have this beautiful little spot carved into the Web, your own decorated online journal with your thoughts and photos for all to see. Now, how do you get readers to stop by? There are several ways to create interest in your blog, from invitations and links to contests and swaps. However, the easiest way is to keep your blog interesting and up to date. If you have the time, post often. People will stop by to see what you are up to if they know you post frequently. Post at least three times a week or more, if possible. Your posts don't always have to include detailed stories of what is going on in your life or business. If you are short on time, or not much is happening that day, a beautiful image with a few lines of text can work just fine and will help your readers feel connected. If you post once a month, don't count on having too many followers.

By Special Invitation

Visiting other blogs you love and sending their authors a personal email to invite them to read your blog is a terrific way to introduce yourself. Would you ignore a new neighbor on your street if she rang your doorbell and asked you to come over and have a cup of tea? Never. I absolutely love to receive these personal invitations.

If someone takes the time to email me a personal invitation, I always stop by the blog to say hello and check it out. If I like what I see, I bookmark the site and make it a frequent stop. Don't be shy about sending a personal email invitation; creative bloggers are warm, generous, and welcoming. Bloggers share their favorite reads by adding links to their blogrolls and writing about and linking to them in posts, so it's important to spread the word about your blog.

Don't

"Hi, my name is Mary. Visit my blog at maryleavesrandomcomments. bloggyblog.com."

Do

"I love your post about your latest vintage discoveries. If you love flea market finds, then you may enjoy my blog, which is all about the hunt. Please visit when you have a chance at maryvintagehunt.blog.com."

In general, when you leave comments on other blogs, it's important to leave your blog link not only so that blog owner can visit, but so their readers can, too. Make sure your comment is not just an advertisement for your own blog; leave a comment that has something to do with their post. Remember that the comment aspect of blogging is what makes it interactive and unique from other types of websites. As you craft your comments, consider how to keep the conversation going. If all you want to convey is "How beautiful!" that is fine. Often your comments are the first impression other bloggers have of you. You want to make sure it is a positive one.

willows95988.typepad.com

I received an email the other day from an American woman (? friend reads my blog. Her friend told her that since she was c France for six months, and since she was going to live close by should contact me.

Corey Amaro made a pact with herself to post to her blog, Tongue in Cheek, every day no matter how busy her life gets.

theblackapple.typepad.com

it was a big hit! I also made her a little monogrammed pen all the precious gel pens (those things are *so* big with the

Artist Emily Martin keeps her readers interested by posting at least three times each week on her blog.

Random Number Generator

This page simply picks a random number, within a range you specify.
For example, to pick a number between 1 and 100, set the *Lowest Number* to be 1, and the *Highest Number* to be 100. Then click on *Pick a Number* to pick the number. That's it. Have fun!

If you found this useful, consider visiting the main Violet Cottage website. Thanks for visiting!

Lowest Number 1
Highest Number

Violets are Blue is the website I use when I need a random number generator. All you have to do is plug in the range of numbers in the correct boxes and click on "Pick a Number."

andrew.hedges.name/experiments/random

Truly Random Number Generator / Picker

Click "Get random!" to pick a random number between 1 and whatever you enter in inclusive. This generates a truly random number by fetching a random seed from Go (Requires JavaScript.)

If you prefer, you can still use the original Random Number Picker.

Enter a number:

I want a number between 1 and...
100

Get random!

Truly Random Number Generator is very easy to use. Because the count automatically starts at 1, you only need to enter the higher number, and then click on Get Number.

And the Winner Is...

Another great way to bring readers to your blog is to have a giveaway. It will attract people as word spreads amongst bloggers who frequent your site that you are having a giveaway. It's also a way to get those lurkers who just read your blog and never comment to come out and say hello.

This is one of my favorite events to host on my blog. I usually try to pull one together at least four or five times a year, and I select a different theme for each one. Having a giveaway is not only fun for the readers, but the host blogger as well. It creates an excitement that can be felt right through the computer screen.

To have a giveaway post, all you need to do is decide what you want to give away. A book? Some vintage finds? The more free things, the better the giveaway. Seriously, who doesn't like free things? Gather up your goodies, and then snap a photo and post with your text about what you are giving away. Invite readers to enter the giveaway by leaving a comment. They can just say "Hello," or "Pick me." Put a timeline on your giveaway (usually three days). When the time's up, close your comments and pick a winner. To do this, you can go the old-fashioned route and put numbers in a hat. (Let's say you had 77 comments, write each number on separate slips of paper, put them in a hat, and pull out a number. If that number is 11, then the 11th person to leave a comment on your post about the giveaway is the winner.) A random number generator is the technological way to do this. These software programs work by generating a random number from a range of numbers entered by the user. To have a computer select a number for you, all you have to do is visit a website that offers this service, enter some numbers, and click on a button.

One of my most successful giveaways had a book theme. The only rule was that readers had to post the title of their favorite book in the comments section. I had more than 300 entries! Once the contest was over, I had this wonderful book list. I wondered, what should I do with it? I created a "Tara & Friends Book Shop" link on my sidebar. The link takes readers to a page where they can see and purchase (from Amazon) the books on the list. Great reads and fun for all! Amazon offers this service, which they call their affiliate program, free of charge. It's called aStore. It took me about five minutes to set it up, and I earn money with every purchase someone makes from my little bookstore link on my sidebar.

Themed Swaps

Similar to a giveaway is a swap. But instead of the host blogger giving something away, she invites bloggers to swap items. Swaps are like gift exchanges; guests sign up and are paired with another guest. After getting to know each other a bit, the two exchange gifts based on the swap's theme. Because participating bloggers post about the swap all the way through and mention the swap in their posts, this is a great way to bring traffic to your blog.

To host a swap, begin with a theme. Kari Ramstrom of Artsy Mama has hosted many successful swaps. Kari says, "The swaps I host are usually holiday related. I host a black-and-white-themed Sweet and Sinister Swap each Halloween. I have done Valentine's Day swaps, a May Day Basket swap, and summer-related swaps. Sometimes the theme is something a bit more open-ended. I once hosted a Vintage Party Swap in which people swapped vintage party supplies on a theme of their choice, for example, a child's birthday party, or wedding."

Once a theme is decided, the swap host posts the theme of the swap, how many people will be accepted, the deadline to sign up (whichever comes first), and the guidelines for the swap including the mailing date for the swap packages to be mailed out to their partner. Visitors who are interested leave a comment on the blog post with their email addresses.

Instead of a giveaway, Alicia Paulson hosted an auction on her blog, Posie Gets Cozy. Half of the proceeds from each doll auctioned went to a different charity.

On her blog, Artsy Mama, Kari Ramstrom hosts a few themed swaps a year. Here is the post about her incredibly successful Vintage Party Swap.

And this towel, my sweet friends, was a dying mistake. When doing some aqua towels, this little guy and a few others, turned out this really pretty green color. I am not sure I can get the exact duplicate again, but please tell me what you think about it. I love the birds! :)

Teresa Sheeley asked readers for their opinion about a towel she created.

Amanda Soule's blog URL matches her blog name. This makes it easy for search engines to find her blog.

When all the participants are gathered, the hostess pairs up partners for the swap. Each pair then gets in touch with one another and gets to know each other better—what they like and dislike as they relate to the items that will be swapped.

Encouraging Comments

Encourage visitors to leave a comment by posting a craft project or idea and asking for their opinions. Bloggers love to give feedback and crafters love receiving it, so it's a win/win situation. Thinking about painting your kitchen Midnight Blue? Take a photo of your room and the paint swatches you are mulling over and ask your readers for help. They'll love to be part of the process and see the finished results as well.

Search Engine Optimization

Search engine optimization, or SEO, is about making sure that search engines can easily find your blog. There are several things you can do to increase your blog's visibility to search engines. (Another reason to think through the naming of your blog.) First, do your best to make sure your blog name is in your URL. For instance, thefarmchicks.typepad.com is the URL for The Farm Chicks blog.

When writing your posts, use great titles. For instance, if you are writing a post about making a pie for a celebration, make sure the title of that post says so. Instead of "My Saturday Morning," your title could be "My Favorite Apple Pie Recipe." Not only will readers be drawn in, but search engines can easily pick out key words. Make sure to repeat those key words, in this instance "apple pie recipe," in your post as well, especially in the first few lines. Posting frequently also helps make your blog visible to search engines by giving them new pages to search.

Links and Blogrolls

Many creative bloggers use links, linkbacks, and blogrolls on their blogs. By linking to other blogs and websites, you increase exposure to your blog, and hopefully increase its readership. Each blog host software platform has a different way of adding these functions to a blog. There are also easy-to-follow tutorials on their websites.

If you want readers to visit another blog or website that you've written about in a post, be sure to create a link to the site in the copy of your blog.

Linkbacks are a method for bloggers to be notified when another blogger links to one of their pages or posts. This lets bloggers keep track of who is linking to their site and referring to their posts, and gives the blogger an idea of who is reading their blog in general.

A blogroll is a way to give exposure to blogs you believe are deserving of attention. A blogroll is a list of links to blogs that focus on topics similar to the ones you focus on in your blog. If you are going to link to another blogger from your site, always ask permission. It's just a little courtesy to say, "Hey, I like your blog. Can I put it on my sidebar?" Ninety-nine percent of the time you will get a "yes." However, don't be insulted if other bloggers do not add your blog since they may not have a blogroll on their site.

Subscriber Feeds

Another way to boost SEO and increase traffic to your blog is to have an RSS feed, also known as a subscriber feed, on your blog. RSS stands for Real Simple Syndication and is a format for delivering to a subscriber's browser or email regularly updated Web content such as blogs. Visitors to your blog can click on the RSS feed link and they will automatically be notified when your blog is updated. Essentially, they are subscribing to receive updates to your blog. RSS links are available free from most Web hosts.

On Crafty Carnival, Missy Ballance has a long list of favorites on her blogroll as well as links to other favorite sites on the Web.

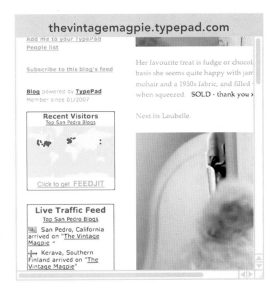

Nicky Fraser makes sure readers can easily find her subscriber feed link on her sidebar when they visit The Vintage Magpie.

Find her: tracithorsonphotography.com/blog
Blogs about: creative endeavors, family life, photography

Traci Thorson started her online journal as a way to capture special moments and the everyday happenings of her family. "Having this blog has taught me that I have a great life," she says. "I tend to blog the positive in my life, which is actually how I view the world. When I read back through the archives, I realize that I am very lucky to be blessed with a wonderful family, great friends, and the ability to share my joys with others."

Traci changes the title on her blog banner often, so she is especially happy that she chose her name as her blog's URL. She explains, "I used my name in the URL and I am glad that I did it that way. At the beginning it was 'Journalings,' then 'Everyday Moments,' then 'Farm-House Studio.' I settled on Traci Thorson Photography Blog because of my passion for photography and the fact that I love including photos with each post."

Making new friends is her favorite thing about blogging. "I love meeting new people," Traci enthuses. "All of the connections I have made with fellow bloggers have enriched my life."

Blogging has also had a positive effect on her online business and has opened the door to new opportunities. "I have an Etsy site where I feature scrapbooking kits and mini albums," says Traci. "Customers have found this shop through my blog."

Traci's most difficult blogging decisions center around her family's privacy. "I have mixed feelings about whether I should have given my husband and kids nicknames on the blog," she says. "Sometimes I feel I should have done that for safety reasons, but that would make my blog less personal. The personal aspect is what I like about my blog."

If you are considering starting your own blog, Traci has a few suggestions. "Include photos, people like visuals," she advises. "Get personal—it draws your visitors in and allows them to get to know you. Don't just be a lurker, leave comments. Comments unite this community."

Traci's favorite daily reads: aliedwards.typepad.com, belladellasfarm.blogspot.com, beckynovacek.typepad.com, karenrussell.typepad.com, thepioneerwoman.com

GRACE BONNEY: Design Sponge

Find her: designspongeonline.com
Blogs about: architecture, house tours, interior design, projects, shopping

When she was little, Grace Bonney soaked up design like a sponge. Now that she's all grown up, this design maven is using her good eye and home design obsession to draw thousands of fans to Design Sponge each day. "I probably should have picked a cooler name," Grace admits. "But then again, I'm not the coolest person, so maybe it's fitting!"

Her blog is a rich blend of content that is almost website-like in its structure. Categories from "Sneak Peeks" to "Mini Trends," and "Before and After" to "DIY," lead readers to postings about designers, cool pads, and great projects from all over the world. Grace does have some freelance help and lots of contributing editors—but she runs the show and blogs daily about "all things design—feminine with a bit of an edge."

Grace comes from a solid background in trends reporting, having worked as a contributing style editor at magazines like Domino, InStyle, and New York Home.

Design Sponge has become one of the most popular blogs covering home design and was dubbed the "Martha Stewart Living of the Millenials" by The New York Times. "I love the ability to post something as soon as it's out," she says. "It really lets you feel like you're on the pulse of what's happening."

Her readers love the house tours, DIY projects, and furniture makeovers. Grace tries to post lots of these, plus stay on top of the hundreds of comments her blog receives. "That's a hard one," she admits. "It's tough to moderate them and find a happy balance between prohibiting inappropriate discussion (cursing, attacking, etc.) and allowing as much freedom of speech as possible."

Still, Grace cannot imagine life without blogging and neither can her 30,000 biggest fans.

Grace's favorite daily reads: mattbites.com, ohjoy.blogs.com

---

guest blog   scholarship   biz ladies *budget *

design sponge*

sneak peeks
mini trends
guides
podcasts
DIY
before & after
categories

FURNITURE

levent and romme

ABBY KERR: Lettres from The Blissful

Find her: theblissful.blogspot.com

Blogs about: daily life, her shop, French décor, special events

Abby Kerr is the owner of The Blissful, a lovely French-inspired home décor boutique in Canton, Ohio. She became a blissful blogger not long after opening her brick-and-mortar store. To capture the feel of her approach to blogging as storytelling through letter writing, she named her new blog space Lettres from The Blissful, spelling "letters" the French way to reflect the identity of her shop.

Captivated by the art of letter writing, Abby set out to create a romantic, epistolary feel on her blog. She considers it a way of writing letters to her customers and hopefully to bloggers around the world.

The blog acts as a virtual catalog of the shop's offerings and coverage of its events, with a mild dose of personal commentary and reflection on shopkeeping and life in general. In a more romantic sense, Abby says, it's a peek into her shop's storefront window. "I like to give a bit of behind-the-scenes info and tales of my trips to market," she explains. "I will also share the frenzy behind the shop's porthole when we close for several days to prepare for special events."

Adds Abby, "Blogging has brought many customers through my doors." She has had people who live close by actually discover the store through her blog. Some have driven in from other states to experience "The Blissful."

Abby's blog advice is to start simply with a template that you like—don't worry about debuting with a fancy custom-designed page. "A new blogger may outgrow a custom blog once she has found her voice and point of view," Abby says.

She also advises to network early and often through blog comments to establish a readership and to make friends. Know your point of view and be true to it. No one else can say it quite like you will, so honor that.

Abby's favorite daily reads: curioussofa.blogspot.com, heatherbullard.typepad.com, theinspiredroom.net

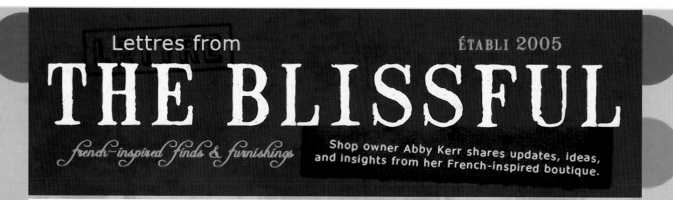

Find her: theblackapple.typepad.com
Blogs about: art, crafts, dollmaking, recipes, shop events

Emily Martin, a painter, illustrator, and dollmaker (she likes to think of herself as an "aspiring Renaissance crafter"), hails from Portland, Oregon. She is also author to one of the most popular blogs in blissful blogdem.

Inside A Black Apple, started in 2006, was a natural off-shoot of Emily's business, "The Black Apple," a collection of her handmade wares. Emily had little more expectation from her blog than as a way to show her mother, a thousand miles away, what she made that day. She also hoped it would allow family and friends to keep up with her daily pursuits when she moved to Brooklyn. "I realized that those close to me are not, in fact, so close with the Internet or with blogs in particular," Emily says. "So the blog grew into its own animal."

The "animal" is now a delightful mix of art-work, crafts, everyday things, shop announcements, projects, recipes, and etceteras. Those etceteras can be found at her Etsy shop (theblackapple.etsy.com), where Emily is ranked as one of the top sellers. She even appeared on "The Martha Stewart Show," teaching the queen of domesticity herself how to make one of her quirky but adorable dolls.

While most readers respond best to her how-to projects, downloadable doll kits, and recipes, Emily finds that they are also incredibly supportive of her other interests. "I love the sharing with like-minded folks who will indulge your waxing on about a vintage button or a children's book," she says.

Emily's advice for bloggers is to try and commit to at least three or four posts per week; the most exciting blogs are the ones that are updated frequently.

Emily's favorite daily reads: angrychicken.typepad.com, kittygenius.com, mypapercrane.com

NEW WORK TO SEE:

Bookin' It

Some mornings I spend hours upon hours at the computer, just

Find her: barij.typepad.com
Blogs about: business, family, life, projects

Bari J. Ackerman, a popular handbag and accessories designer, began blogging in 2007. Her self-titled blog lets her announce business news, offer fun projects, share pictures and stories from everyday life, and give information and inspiration to women entrepreneurs.

She describes her blog as "colorful, authentic, fun, and inspiring." Bari's main focus is to just be herself when it comes to blogging. She tells stories of her family and life, exactly as it is, and as she says, "It's not all cupcakes and roses."

"Often, as women, we think that other people are better at this or that, their home is always clean, their laundry is always done, and dinners are always homemade," Bari says. "We place impossible standards of perfection upon ourselves by using this line of thought."

Bari wants her blog to demonstrate that everyone makes mistakes and faces challenges. It's also important to her to present that what she calls "a pretty, pretty life" is not all it's cracked up to be. Her honesty and candor has made her blog a favorite among many blissful bloggers. They love that she shares the good, the bad, and the ugly with her readers.

She says she doesn't want her blog to be all about pitching herself and her products. Bari's posts intertwine her everyday life and her business in a beautiful combination that keeps readers coming back for more. People respond the most to her posts about personal stories and challenges.

Her blog has allowed Bari to meet an incredible amount of people, which has helped her business. She says the support and encouragement received on a daily basis cannot be measured. Taking the time to write about what is going on in her life and business has forced her to think more and slow down.

Bari's advice for the new blogger? "Be real, put a photo on every post, and no dirty laundry," she says.

Bari's favorite daily reads: afancifultwist.typepad.com, annamariahorner.blogspot.com, yummygoods.com

DEBBIE DUSENBERRY: Curious Sofa Diaries

Find her: curioussofa.blogspot.com

Blogs about: business, home décor, special events

Debbie Dusenberry, owner of the well-known Curious Sofa home décor shop in Kansas City, Kansas, started her blog, Curious Sofa Diaries, as a way to keep customers up to date on what's happening in the shop. Curious Sofa does not sell merchandise online, so Debbie saw this avenue as a means to keep her news fresh and customers informed.

Debbie's achieved all that and more. Local press and word-of-mouth referrals have brought many customers to the blog, but it's the national press that shot her visibility "through the roof." Says Debbie, "I'll post a photo of a new item on my blog and immediately I get emails and phone calls about buying it."

Curious Sofa Diaries has a very simple design. Debbie decided not to have blogrolls, links, or advertisements. Her focus is on the central message of each post, and she considers her blog to be an adjunct to her store, plain and simple.

The best part about blogging, Debbie happily confides, is savoring the relationships that are built with her fans and the comments she receives from business owners over the trouble they all face. It helps her to know she is not alone.

Debbie advises aspiring bloggers to be nice when posting with their comments, realizing the purpose of each individual blog. "A basic 'good job!' is enough to write for your comment," she says, adding that you should really read the entry before commenting. "It's obvious when someone is rambling on just to get posted so others see her own blog—and that's tacky."

The Author

Of course, New York

MALKA DUBRAWSKY: A Stitch in Dye

Find her: stitchindye.blogspot.com

Blogs about: crafting, fabric dyeing, her travels, photography, quilting, sewing

Malka Dubrawsky is not your ordinary textile artist. She breathes life into ordinary fabrics by dyeing and patterning them, and then uses the fabrics to create extraordinary quilts, pillows, table runners, and more. She had an established business, A Stitch in Dye, so when she started her blog in 2006, she gave it the same name.

At first, Malka envisioned her blog as a place to talk about her life, passions, and thoughts, but now it is focused on her business. Malka says, "My blog is almost entirely about my work. It's been a venue for me to promote my work and to explore my interest in photography."

Beautiful photography is a hallmark of Malka's blog, and it's something she works at and enjoys. Her bright, colorful fabrics are showcased in every post in images that are rich and inviting. "I think what makes my blog unique is the work that I showcase," she explains. "I also post quality photographs—I'm a very visually oriented person and I think that's apparent in my blog." She also feels it's important to keep a friendly and welcoming voice when writing her posts.

The technical side of blogging has, at times, been a thorn in her side. A limited knowledge of how to customize her blog has often left her feeling frustrated. When asked what she would do differently with her blog, Malka says, "I think I would learn a little more about HTML so that I could manipulate the features of my blog without always having to rely on my husband. Also, if I really understood the code behind the blog I'd know what the possibilities are and could make creative decisions based on that."

The benefits of blogging far outweigh any small frustration. "Professionally, my blog and through it my connection to the photo sharing site, Flickr, has brought me an amazing amount of opportunities," Malka says. "Personally, I have so enjoyed the comments and interactions with readers that I wouldn't have had it not been for my blog."

For anyone thinking about starting a blog, Malka shares the following advice: Post the best quality pictures you have. Look around. See what you like and don't like about other blogs and work with that knowledge. Mostly, though, do it because you think it will be fun for you.

Malka's favorite daily reads: brooklyntweed.blogspot.com, designspongeonline.com, yarnharlot.ca/blog

a stitch in dye

Find her: homespunliving.blogspot.com
Blogs about: family, knitting, life, sewing

When her kids went off to college and jobs a few years ago, Debbie Andriulli was facing an empty nest. Over the years she and her children had shared many creative endeavors. "I hoped my blog would provide a new creative outlet and help to connect me with other like-minded women," she says. "The real joy of creating comes from having someone with whom to share it."

Her little corner in blogdom, Homespun Living, looks at the simple pleasures in life. In her posts, Debbie shares her latest projects, recipes, flea market finds, and more. She says, "I like to hope that it is a peaceful and comfortable spot to visit and that visitors can take away something useful."

Debbie's biggest blogging challenge is writing. She says, "Writing is not my strong point, particularly writing about myself. I am not good at articulating my thoughts, and so it takes me much too long to write a post. Therefore, my entries are usually short; I rely on my pictures to help make up for that."

Her readers, though, love her posts. "Entries are often inspired by my latest sewing, knitting, crafting, or home improvement project," says Debbie. "Sometimes I write about my nature walks or life on our little farm—there is always lots of inspiration there—a delivery of new baby chicks, picking blackberries for jam, the garden harvest, or horseback riding. Posts about 'Corners of My Home,' projects, and patterns have received a good response. But, I received the most comments by far when I posted of my dad's illness and passing—the kind words and consolation offered by readers was heartwarming."

Blogging did not come easy for Debbie, however. She says, "In the beginning I was very apprehensive. Would people be nice? Would they care about what I had to share? It was almost three months before I got the courage to make my blog public. At most, I hoped to hear from a few women who shared similar interests."

Her courage and patience paid off. "I did not anticipate that so many visitors would come by from all over the world," says Debbie. "Blogging has helped me realize the potential I have, that any of us have as individuals, to touch the lives of others and perhaps even make a difference in the world."

Debbie's favorite daily reads: sewmamasew.com/blog2, petitsdetails.com, eyes-of-wonder.blogspot.com, storybookwoods.typepad.com, mommycoddle.typepad.com

homespun
living

Chapter 6   FINDING
••••• **BUSINESS**
IN
••••• **BLISS**

There are many creative bloggers who have made the transition from pleasure to profit. Some of them started blogging for pleasure and saw their ideas blossom into an unforeseen, successful business. Others started blogging as a way to share tips, ideas, and projects, and a few created blogs to simply showcase online businesses, or brick-and-mortar stores. Whatever road they took, their journeys have been successful in more ways than one. These bloggers have built blogs that create loyal followers and solid businesses.

Talking About Business

So you have something to sell and want to tell your blog readers. Many crafty bloggers have a link on their website featuring their eBay store or Etsy site. This is one great, subtle way to show off your wares. Blogging for business can also be as easy as posting about your latest item for sale and blending it with a story of how a particular item was made. Keep in mind that your readers don't like a hard sell; it's best to talk about the chaos that got you to the creation, and save the hard-sell information for a store newsletter.

Your type of creative business will help determine the best way to promote your commerce through your blog. Are you a graphic designer? Make sure your blog design is spectacular, write about your services on your profile page, and include links to your design website and samples of your work. Include testimonials with the samples. Write about your design business on your blog.

If you are a photographer, take a cue from the tips for the graphic designer; additionally, make sure to include amazing images with every blog post. You may also consider giving free tutorials about working with images as one of your blog categories. Bloggers love to learn new things, especially if the information is free.

Are you a writer, consultant, or guest speaker? Include stories of your professional life on your creative blog, and include links to pages about the services you offer. If you blog about your real brick-and-mortar interior design retail store, tell readers about recent product arrivals or upcoming special events. Another way to build loyal readership is to include tips on decorating or entertaining in your posts.

Debbie Dusenberry of Curious Sofa Diaries always posts spectacular images of design ideas to inspire her readers. Give your readers interesting stories and something of value—you will build a dedicated readership and loyal customer base.

Curious Sofa Diaries is where Debbie Dusenberry talks about her store and dispenses decorating and entertaining advice.

Alys Geertsen uses her blog, Paris Couture Antiques, to showcase products and store events relating to her hugely successful retail store.

Jennifer Perkins features BlogHer ads on her blog, Naughty Secretary Club. Since the ads are targeted toward her readers, there is no negative reaction to them.

Design Sponge is a great example of a blog that has had success using Google ads. This works because every ad appeals to the blog's readers.

Blogvertising

Historically, creative bloggers have not been very accepting of ads on blogs. Some bloggers feel that if you accept ads on your blog, you no longer blog from your heart, or that you aren't blogging just for the pleasure of writing and connecting with others. That you are a sellout. But those viewpoints are changing. More creative bloggers are running ads on their sites and bloggers are becoming more accepting of them. Some bloggers have more success than others running ads on their sites. Why? They always consider their audience before accepting any type of ad. Another thing to think about is that the amount of income you make from the ads on your blog most likely isn't going to pay the rent, so don't dream about quitting your day job.

There are a couple of different types of ads on blogs: pay-per-click and impression. An impression ad appears on a blog's sidebar. The term impression refers to page views. Every time a reader visits a blog that has an impression ad, software records that page visit as an impression. Bloggers who have impression ads are paid by an estimation of many times an ad is viewed.

With pay-per-click ads, bloggers are paid in relation to how many times visitors to their blog click on the ad. Special software programs measure the amount of times an ad is clicked on versus how many times it is viewed.

Google AdSense matches ads to your blog site's content and audience, and depending on the type of ad, you can earn money from clicks or impressions. Google provides the ads so you don't have to worry about interacting with the advertisers. To apply for Google AdSense, you must have a blog with acceptable content and a valid URL, as well as a valid payee name and mailing address to receive your payments.

BlogHer is another popular advertising service, and all of their ads are geared toward women. They offer CPM (cost per 1,000 impressions) ads. Once you sign up and are accepted, you will be able to choose the type and size of ads that will run on your blog. If you decide to discontinue advertising on your blog, BlogHer allows you to opt out with a 30-day notice. They do have limited openings for new bloggers in their advertising network, so you may be put on a waiting list.

Claire Robinson is happy to run ads on her blog, Loobylu. She says, "I don't even think about them really and I certainly don't let the presence of advertising on my blog affect what I have to say in my blog posts. I think it's a perfectly wonderful way for someone to make an income. If it means that people can financially justify the time it takes to keep up a good blog, and they are able to happily keep blogging on about whatever they want to blog about without compromising for, or pandering to, their advertisers, then fabulous!"

Here are a few things to avoid if you do decide to run ads on your creative blog:

- Blinkies—Does anyone like those annoying blinking advertisements?
- Ads with sound—Another irritating no-no.
- Ads that are too large, or that have no connection to you or your readers' interests.

Affiliate Programs

The term affiliate marketing refers to a revenue-sharing plan where an online automated marketing program lets bloggers place an advertiser's ads or buttons on their site. Blog owners receive a referral fee or commission from conversions (a conversion is when a customer has clicked the affiliate link and performs the desired action, such as make a purchase on the advertiser's site). Amazon and Borders' affiliate programs are free to join and have no set-up fee. You simply post their ad or a link to their products on your blog's sidebar, and every time a conversion occurs on your blog you get paid a commission. This option works well with creative bloggers because the products the companies offer are mainly books and music.

Google AdSense is a program for website publishers (including bloggers) to display relevant, unobtrusive Google ads on their site and earn money.

My "Tara & Friends Book Shop" is set up through Amazon.com's affiliate program.

REBECCA SOWER: Rebecca Sower's Weblog

Find her: rebeccasower.typepad.com

Blogs about: crafting, everyday life, mixed-media art, photography, poetry

Rebecca Sower likes to keep things simple—from her blog name to the designs and posts she features. Her site, which she describes as "creatively inspirational," swoops and soars like a bird from a short poem about nature's sparing use of yellow to waxing rhapsodic on a pair of handknit socks. When she went on vacation one summer, Rebecca treated readers to a "photo a day," a terrific way to take a blog break. Readers can take a stroll through her incredible photography, or perhaps stop by her Etsy shop, where she sells her mixed-media artwork.

Pulling together art, quotes, and poetry, Rebecca weaves a tapestry of story and images that captures her musings in an extraordinary way. Blogging has allowed Rebecca to observe her surroundings as if seeing them through her readers' eyes, further adding to the beauty around her. "Sometimes I struggle to post every day and then I remember how important my readers are to me," Rebecca says. "That makes it much easier to get motivated."

There are two approaches to blissful blogging, Rebecca says. One is a diary style, where you reflect on everyday life. The other is more inspirational in nature, where you seek to instruct, impassion, and satisfy readers looking for ways to improve their own lives. "I think it would be hard to do both," she says.

Inspiration is definitely the thing Rebecca gives in droves to her many faithful readers.

Rebecca's favorite daily reads: housewrenstudio. typepad.com, ornamental.typepad.com, teresamcfay den.typepad.com

Welcome...

GABREIAL WYATT: Vintage Indie

Find her: vintageindie.typepad.com

Blogs about: collecting, crafting, independent artists, projects

Monday morning makes most of us groan and reach for the snooze button. But for Gabreial Wyatt, it's nothing less than joyous. "I love Mondays," she says. "It's important to start off fresh and aim for high goals of joy and prosperity for the week."

Gabreial, the brainchild behind the Vintage Indie blog, taps into the world of creative individuals who also have a passion for old school goods. It began in 2007 when Gabreial sold her bath, body, and spa company and was brainstorming ideas of what she was most passionate about. She knew she wanted to return to her love of writing. So her list began with "vintage" as the main topic of interest. Next on the list was her passion for supporting the independent small business (better known as "indie") as she was once one herself. Gabreial combined these two things to create the Vintage Indie concept.

The blog is a daily dose of vintage, collectibles, and handmade goods. It showcases independent sellers, designers, and store owners as well as their buyers. She also features DIY projects, home tours, and interviews.

Personally, Gabreial says, the blog is a place to come with a cup of coffee or tea and enjoy modern life with a vintage perspective—a relaxing place to shop for vintage and handmade items that you won't find in the "big box" stores.

Vintage Indie accepts advertisements, but they must be submitted by indie crafters. Gabreial has created a wonderful visual balance so that the blog has not become too commercialized in appearance. The ads are well-placed and most importantly, they are designed beautifully. The blog itself is very pleasing to the eye, and Gabreial says it's been a goal of hers to keep it as entertaining and indie friendly as possible.

"I feel that the creative blogging community is full of strangers doing good for each other," she says. "I am motivated by the designers who dare to make something different with their own hands."

Gabreial's favorite daily reads: blog.caseybrownde signs.com, rocksinmydryer.typepad.com, lazyorganizer. com/blog

Vintage Indie
Modern Life ✦ Vintage Perspective

TERESA SHEELEY: Teresa Sheeley

Find her: teresaksheeley.typepad.com

Blogs about: art, daily life, design, studio happenings

Teresa Sheeley, a watercolor artist and greeting card designer, began her blog in 2006. Her goal was to create a blog where art and life inspire. Teresa admits she was apprehensive about putting her first pieces of art out there for the world to see. The process of blogging, however, lifted that fear and gave her more confidence in her abilities as an artist.

Her blog entries are inspired by little things in her daily life. Ordinary life becomes extraordinary, with a snap of Teresa's camera and a few words. Her readers respond mostly to something new she has made or if she is having a giveaway. One topic that spurred a lot of comment was her political views. While the debate was lively, Teresa didn't want her creative space to become a place for political rants, so she quickly changed direction and continued posting her artwork and life from her studio.

Blogging has helped Teresa grow as a person, giving her initiative, inspiration, and more self-esteem. It also has helped her business grow—Teresa linked her Etsy store to her blog and lets readers know when she has something new. "My blog is the No. 1 reason for my business success," she says. "It's a great tool for getting started and showcasing what you can do as an artist."

Her advice for new bloggers: Explore lots of other blogs, and then study the different platforms carefully before you select one. Most importantly, Teresa says, is to stay true to yourself. "We each have a special voice that can be heard and ideas we are wishing to share with others," she says. "Blogging is a wonderful place to do it."

Teresa takes advantage of how easy it is to shake things up on her blog by frequently changing its look. From different banners to new colors and layouts, she continually delights her readers with the unexpected.

Teresa's favorite daily reads: churningsandburnings.blogspot.com, sadieolive.typepad.com, willows95988.typepad.com

Teresa Sheeley

JENNIFER PERKINS: Naughty Secretary Club

Find her: naughtysecretaryclub.blogspot.com

Blogs about: business, crafting, jewelry design, personal life

When Jennifer Perkins started her business creating and selling jewelry, she was still employed as a secretary. "I was supposed to be filing," she confesses. "That's when I came up with the name—I figured there were other naughty secretaries out there like me."

Jennifer has been blogging since 2005, and considers her blog an extension of her business. As a jewelry maker, author, craft host, and member of the Austin Craft Mafia, she needs to make every minute count. As a new mother, Jennifer says, "The challenge will be to find the time and the urge to write. I also don't want to turn my blog into a personal diatribe about how cute my kid is. It will be hard to find a balance, but I am determined to do it."

Everything about Naughty Secretary Club makes it stand out amidst creative blogs, from the name to the topics it covers. Take, for instance, something like "Taxi-

dermy Trends." Deer heads mounted on a wall doesn't sound very crafty but when you look at the ingenious interpretations with knitting and paper on the blog, you'll no doubt change your mind. Naughty Secretary Club is filled with great crafting ideas, ways to use jewelry as a decorating element, and glimpses here and there of Jennifer's personal life.

Although many blog readers don't like seeing ads, Jennifer's decision to accept ads doesn't keep her awake at night. "I look at blogs with ads and they never bother me," she says. "If you are going to take the time to find a topic, take pictures, write about it, and post, then you should be getting paid for your work."

Jennifer's favorite daily reads: design-crisis.com, stylebubble.typepad.com, themoldydoily.typepad.com, westcoastcrafty.wordpress.com

CAROL SPINSKI: Raised in Cotton

Find her: raisedincotton.typepad.com
Blogs about: business, crafting, projects, shopping

Carol Spinski started a blog in 2005 to drive business to her new brick-and-mortar shop of the same name. She had a strong vision of how she wanted her blog to grow; she also knew that creative blogging was the wave of the future. Following her instinct has certainly paid off—within three years of launching her online journal, Carol's early shop announcements evolved into a favorite daily stop for blog readers worldwide.

Carol's blog, which she says "celebrates leading a creative lifestyle by offering fresh and simple ideas," is a chronicling of her own personal journey, as well as a vehicle to share the multitude of ideas that are constantly swirling around in her artistic mind.

The name Raised in Cotton comes from an old Southern term meaning to be born with a silver spoon in your mouth; for Carol, it means to spoil yourself and beautify your surroundings. To spoil her readers and keep them coming back for more, Carol shares crafting tips and how-to projects with step-by-step instructions

at least once a month, in her trademark vintage style. Every post is accompanied by beautiful images.

Carol tries to set aside one or two days a week to post and keep her blog fresh, and she says her entries are inspired by bits and pieces of things she collects while searching for treasures—old architectural pieces, for example. She admits she feels guilty (as most bloggers do) that she can't post as often as she would like, since she has a business to run.

Carol's advice to new bloggers is to decide what you want to convey with your blog before starting. Respond to the people who take time to leave a comment, even if it's a simple two-word email that says, "Thank you." She also advises that rather than being a complainer, be humble and friendly. In addition, offer helpful information, such as an idea, project, or tip, on a regular basis.

Carol's favorite daily reads: curioussofa.blogspot. com, decor8blog.com, heatherbullard.typepad.com, karlascottage.typepad.com, sadieolive.typepad.com

JENNIFER PAGANELLI: Sis Boom

Find her: jenniferpaganelli.typepad.com
Blogs about: design, fabrics, home décor

Based on a childhood nickname and her fabric line, Jennifer Paganelli's Sis Boom blog began in 2005 as "a way to let people see the fabrics at work." Originally, Jennifer wanted a blog to help people understand what her design aesthetic was all about. Sis Boom, she says, has always been difficult to describe and she wanted to show what vintage-inspired really meant. Her "visual dictionary" turned out to be much more and emerged as a wildly popular blog read by people who wanted to add a little Sis Boom to their own lives.

The design philosophy behind Sis Boom is pairing old and new elements, and actually emphasizing the imperfections. When the fragility of the old meets the youthful fun of Sis Boom's signature bold colors, a new relevance emerges. "There is a sense of well-being when things can harmonize comfortably," Jennifer says. She feels blessed that there are so many folks who love what they are doing and can now create the look with fabrics that reference the past—and best of all, she can see it all and talk about it on her blog.

Jennifer's blog is not all about fabrics and patterns. She reveals snippets of daily life with an engaging honesty and she loves the comments that come back, proof that women who go through similar events (some good, some bad) will rally around in support.

Her blog has taught her that her fear of nothing to share is a silly notion. She has met so many talented women who all learn from one another. "It's a fellowship, truly," she says.

Jennifer's only regret on her blog journey? Not asking for the digital SLR camera a few Christmases ago. "A good camera is a creative blogger's best friend," she says.

Jennifer's favorite daily reads: everyday-is-a-holiday. blogspot.com, grandrevivaldesign.typepad.com

BENITA LARSSON: Chez Larsson

Find her: chezlarsson.typepad.com

Blogs about: decorating, DIY projects, entertaining, shopping

An emphasis on clean, white, affordable, organized, Scandinavian living gives a unique focus to Benita Larsson's blog. Her posts often feature home restoration and decorating projects she tackles with her husband on a regular basis. "We live in a 1930s self-build and as with all houses and homes, there's no such thing as finishing," says Benita, a visual merchandiser who resides in Sweden. "One thing leads to another and another and another. Organizing is my forte. It's not my profession but I've loved it ever since I was a little girl, when I would help my mom organize her cabinets and drawers."

Benita says she gets a lot of satisfaction seeing the before and after of a project. "My husband once said that if there was an event called 'organizing' in the Olympics, I'd win it," she says. "I've also been called the MacGyver of decorating by one of my readers. I loved that."

Benita has a particular knack for solving decorating issues with what's on hand and is able to do it in an aesthetically pleasing manner. "I've realized that I'm actually helping my readers get more organized and that inspires me to give them even more," she enthuses.

Visitors to her blog respond the most to her posts about decorating and organizing. "I love reading in the comments that a reader has finally gotten inspired to organize this or that area around her/his home and even enjoyed it."

The name of her blog loosely translated from French means, "At the Larssons." Though she likes the name, Benita says she wishes she would've given it a bit more thought. "Not everybody understands that Chez is not my first name and I often get emails saying 'Hi Chez,'" she says. "I also think I should have added the word 'organizing' in there somewhere but people seem to find me regardless so it's no big deal."

After years in the corporate world, Benita has been able to cut back her work hours to pursue her own creative projects. To offset her reduction in income, she accepts a few ads on her site. "I'm not making huge amounts, but every little bit helps," she says.

The most difficult thing about blogging for Benita has been the time it takes away from her family. "I sometimes feel I am in front of the computer far too many hours a day," she says. "They are very much behind me, though, and are totally understanding, which does make it easier."

Benita's favorite daily reads: aliedwards.typepad.com, doorsixteen.com, makingitlovely.com, yvestown.com

Chez Larsson A blog about house, home & hobbies

MISSY BALLANCE: Crafty Carnival

Find her: missyballance.typepad.com
Blogs about: crafting, family

Missy Ballance comes from a long line of crafty women. As a result, Missy says, "My blog is a great big mish-mash of all things crafty. While sewing is my favorite medium, I really love to work in many different aspects of craft."

When she started her blog, one of Missy's intentions was to have it complement her mohair bear business (Mohair Circus), but not limit it to just bears. Crafty Carnival is her perfect solution. Asked if she would ever consider changing the name of her blog, Missy quickly replies, "No, I think the name fits perfectly, and it's just trendy enough. I love my blog name."

When Missy began her blog, her intentions were to share her crafty inspirations, along with things she makes or attempts to make. Missy explains her reasoning: "I wanted to share both my failures and successes in hopes of encouraging others to do the same."

Now she finds that her blog has become more than just a place to talk about crafts and family; it has changed her outlook on many things. "Blogging has made me feel like I'm a part of a bigger thing," she says. "I don't know what that 'thing' is. It's kind of indescribable. But as a woman who crafts, takes care of kids, and tries to 'do it all,' blogging has made me feel that I'm appreciated. I'm a part of this bigger group of people who appreciate each other because in some small way we are all trying to 'do it all' together."

For Missy, the most difficult part about blogging is saying no to other artists. "I get a lot of requests from artists to feature them on my blog," she explains. "It is hard for me to feature other people's work on my blog because then it's no longer my blog, it's just one big advertisement. I like to write about things I've found on the Internet or am inspired by, but I don't like to be solicited to do so. It's not that I don't want to help other artists, because I do. I've found the best solution is to offer advice, or offer to help others start their own blogs. This is more helpful than me featuring them one time anyway."

When it comes to actual advertising, Missy has decided to feature Google ads for now, and only because doing so helps cover the cost of running her blog. She says, "I think it justifies the fact that I spend almost $100 per year to host my blog and have it look pretty."

Missy's favorite daily reads: abeautifulmess.typepad.com, geeksugar.com, mylittlemochi.typepad.com

Chapter 7
····· IF EMILY...
POST(ED)

Remember Emily? She reigned supreme in the Manners Manor long before blogging was a verb, or even a word. "Don't write a letter when you're angry," she would say. Or, "Always send a thank-you after visiting someone, whether for business or pleasure."

Emily's pursuit of civility lives on at the Emily Post Institute, run by third-generation family members, but it seems that her well-chosen words of wisdom often go unheeded on the wild, wild Web.

Since we are most interested in the realm of crafting and art, most of the following advice stems from comments made by fellow crafty bloggers. Just like their posts are filled with feelings and opinions, their readers have their own feelings (and opinions in palooza proportions). I've polled hundreds of readers on my own blog

and asked them to express some of their pet peeves. The results are interesting and thought provoking, as you will see. Overall, while I expected to see some of the answers, others were quite surprising.

Manners Matter

Many of the basic civilities and manners drilled into us as kids are utterly relevant in the blogging community and should be dusted off and minded when we blog or post comments.

Banish Blog Snobs

We all remember the popular cliques in high school. We may have been part of one—or not. Be sensitive to your readers and include them in the big party at your house. In other words, take the time to type a few words and create a linkback to new visitors. A reader takes valuable time to read your post then comment and they want you to visit their blog in return.

Me, Myself, and I

Keep in mind that no one likes a braggart. There are ways to tell your readers that your husband just bought you a new convertible for your birthday without looking like a superficial reality TV star. Mix exciting news within an everyday post and your readers will be sure to appreciate it more. Also, readers don't like posts that are nothing but a hard shove into your online boutique. They won't come back if it's just one big advertisement, post after post. So break up those announcements and be humble.

The same holds true for always posting how busy you are. Remember, we are all busy; while we are reading your blog, there are kids fighting in the next room, a pot of water is boiling on the stove, and the dog is scratching at the back door. If you need to take a break from your blog, just post an announcement telling your readers when you will be back.

The Farm Chicks, Serena Thompson and Teri Edwards, believe in the power of positivity. In this post they write about supporting fellow artists and crafters.

Holly Becker created Decor8 as a way to showcase the creative endeavors of others. With her blog, she is a shining example of sharing good things.

Though her site has all kinds of bells and whistles, Zee Longnecker makes sure her site loads quickly.

Like many bloggers, Kasey Buick likes having music on her blog. Do your readers a favor and make sure that the volume button is easy to find.

Behind the Scenes

There are a few things you can take care of in the set-up stage of your blog (or as you add features) to ensure that readers enjoy visiting your site. Your blog may be about *your* life, but you should always remember that you are creating something for the enjoyment of others.

Noises off

We all love music and carry our MP3 players in their fancy cases, but a majority of blog readers don't want your favorite tune blaring at them. One woman said she surfs creative blogs late at night while nursing her baby and sometimes the music scares her (and the baby). If you must have your music and play it too, instrumental music is preferred, and definitely have an easy-to-find off button.

Spam prevention

Spammers menace the blogosphere just as they do your email accounts. Sometimes spam comes from disgruntled bloggers who enjoy leaving very negative or offensive comments. Comment spam can also be generated by software programs. In the blogosphere they are know as spambots. A spambot is a type of Web crawler software program or automated script that browses the World Wide Web in a methodical, automated manner. This process is called Web crawling or spidering. Many websites, especially search engines, use Web crawling as a means of providing up-to-date data.

Spambots are the delinquents of the Web crawlers. They surf the Web, looking for guest books, wikis, blogs, forums, and any other Web forms to submit spam links to the Web forms (such as blog comment fields). Some spam messages are targeted toward readers and can involve target marketing or even phishing, making it hard to tell real posts from the spambot-generated ones. Not all of the spam posts are meant for the readers; some really harmful spam messages are simply hyperlinks intended to boost search engine ranking. So on top of being annoying, spambots are actually harmful. By leaving spam comments, spambots make your blog unappealing to search engines. If you want to prevent spam comments on your blog, there are some simple software solutions available.

Many of my blogging friends tell me, "I can't stand typing in those code thingies just to leave a comment." That would be CAPTCHA verification and it works by generating and grading tests that humans can pass but current computer programs cannot. You've used CAPTCHA verification every time you've had to type in those crazy-looking letters and numbers in order to access a website. A free download of the software can be accessed through the CAPTCHA website (captcha. net). Most popular blog software has this feature built in or available as a plug-in, so make sure to check your blog's support tools for help. Though it can be a bit frustrating for your readers, using this type of verification will prevent spam comments.

Another option is to have readers sign in to leave a comment. I do not recommend this. By making the process difficult, readers are less likely to leave comments.

Because spambots often have the ability to bypass any CAPTCHAs present, you may want to consider using filtering software, a behind-the-scenes option to prevent comment spam. These programs run continuously and require very little of your time for set-up or maintenance. Most blog hosts offer a filtering program as part of their basic service. I highly recommend using this feature on your blog. By preventing spam from reaching your blog comments, this software ensures the integrity of your blog. This is important because if your blog comments are full of spam, search engines are much less likely to include your blog in search results.

Filtering software runs tests on comments to determine whether they are valid or spam. Comments determined to be spam are then put in a database where you can review and post them if they are indeed valid comments. You also can block comments containing certain

CAPTCHA, those crazy letters and numbers you have to type in a bar, is one way to prevent spam comments on your blog.

Most blog hosts provide spam filtering software at no additional cost, as seen here on WordPress.

Happy Harris writes her blog in her native language, English, but offers the Google translation widget on her sidebar.

Here is the same post as seen above, only it has been translated into Italian. Notice that the graphics and images have remained the same.

words or that are from certain IP addresses. If your service doesn't offer comment filtering, you can easily download filtering software. Akismet is the most popular download of this type and is free for personal use. You can download it from akismet.com.

Please wait to be seated

We are talking load time here, and I don't mean laundry. When someone stops by your blog and they have to wait a long time for it to appear on their computer screen, they may decide to leave you for the next blog.

Speed it up by archiving your posts (I recommend only 10 posts per page). This is a simple fix in the blog set-up (see Chapter 4). Don't know if your blog loads fast enough? Ask your readers! You don't want to be known as a slowsky. Sidebar fancies can slow up the blog as well, so resize them (see Chapter 4) and get your blog freely flowing once again.

Junk in the trunk

Although some sidebar fancies can be pretty and well done, having too many on your blog can be visually distracting. When designing your blog, make sure your sidebars are not overloaded with features. Also, most readers don't want to see blinkies and giant billboards. Leave that to the highways, not your blog.

Translation Services

Blissful blogging is a worldwide phenomenon. No matter what language a blogger writes in, they will most likely have followers in other countries. In recognition of this, translation services are now available. Google, for instance, has a sidebar translation widget. All a reader has to do is select their language from a drop-down menu, and the translated page is reloaded in seconds. Graphics and images are unchanged. WordPress also offers a translation add-on.

Take a Picture, Please

We all want to connect in some way—that's why we read blogs. So don't hide behind your pet's photo or a random picture of a flower. Readers want to see who you are and they want the information at the top of your blog where it's easy to spot.

Some bloggers are nervous about showing themselves on the Internet. You have to decide how comfortable you feel about revealing yourself, dyed roots and all, to people. You're already baring your soul about your husband's annoying new habit, your latest craft project, shopping habits, or how you forgot to tip the waiter at last night's dinner outing.

Other Bones to Pick

- Typos and bad grammar—use the spell checker!
- TYPING IN ALL CAPS, which makes readers feel like they are being yelled at.
- Tag, you're it. Though they are popular, tag awards and such should be avoided. If you have a blog, you know what I'm talking about. We all secretly hate them as they are similar to the dreaded chain mail. Break the chain, it won't bring you bad luck.
- Don't make mom wash your mouth out with soap. Foul language on a creative blog is a bad, bad thing. I was really surprised at how frequently this occurs. Because creative blogs are so visual, this is really like seeing profane graffiti spray-painted on your driveway. Not cool.
- Overly long posts. Keep your posts short, sweet, and to the point. One savvy blogger suggested that if you are going to be long-winded, break up your giant paragraph into two or three sections. Embellish freely with photos.
- Readers love animals, but too many posts about your pets and they'll feel like they are at the zoo.

Charlotte Lyon's About Me page includes a brief biography and links to her email, contact information, and Etsy site. Of course, she included her photo.

Monica Solorio-Snow keeps her posts interesting and easy to read by including great images and breaking copy into short sections.

bushelandapeck.typepad.com

I do a lot more cooking than baking. I just don't take the time to bake enough to really get great at it. I have so many friends that are phenomenal bakers that they even bless me with cakes on my birthday. It is sad how much of the cakes I can eat by myself! I can handle a crisp though! What really sets this crisp apart from others I have made is the orange zest and the Grand Marnier......yum. Enjoy! If you make it let me know how it turns out.

4 cups diced rhubarb

4 cups fresh strawberries, hulled, and halved, if large

1 cup granulated sugar

2 teaspoons orange zest

2 tablespoons cornstarch

A great example of an interesting post, this recipe was featured on Jeanne Griffin's blog.

ravenhill.typepad.com

Emily Fletcher Moss is an amazing artist and photographer and makes sure to give readers the eye candy they crave on her blog, Ravenhill.

- To all you lurkers and lookie-loos: Leave a comment! Blog posts take time and thought. Your comments are appreciated by the blog owner and most of us read every single one. I know I try to email or visit the blog link left by readers to let them know I appreciate them. It's a really nice way to say thank you.

On Your Way

Beginning to blog is an exciting time. The world is at your fingertips. Eventually you will find your voice and your audience. Sometimes your words will come from a photograph or you will write the words and find a photo to express your post later. We are all storytellers in our own unique way. I hope this book has taught you how to blog from the heart. Blog about what you love and the rest will fall into place. Take time to see and notice the small things in your day and appreciate them. Others will too.

Remember that blogging is not a chore or obligation but an option to express your thoughts, feelings, crafts, and projects, whether related to family, work, home, or all three. You get to decide how much of your life to put on the screen. It's your story, your words, your vision, your life. Because blogging is a two-way street, remember to invite your readers to share in the experience. Ask their opinions, request their advice, respond to their comments. Your blogging experience will be more rewarding if you do.

We are all creative creatures, soaking in inspiration. We pass on the inspiration to others and the creative circle continues. Blogging will become a natural part of your routine and soon you will be blogging for bliss. One of the wonderful things about blogs is how they endure. Long after this book is printed, my blog will live on. I would love to see the blogs you build, hear about how you progress in the journey, and answer your questions. I am here in my pink fuzzy slippers, typing out loud (tara-frey.com), and waiting to hear from you. So please visit anytime.

Find her: amusements.typepad.com

Blogs about: collections, creating, friends, her artwork, her life

Karen Otto has a refined ability to see beauty in every aspect of her life. She was an interior designer for 15 years, and has taught classes in assemblage, collage, and polymer clay, but she loves all things paper. "I would imagine that the closest definition of my art is mixed-media," she says. "My artwork has been shown at The Sundance Film Festival, The Boise Art Museum, Mary Lou Zeek Gallery, and in shops across the country." Karen's blog has the same name as her art business, and is the place where she shares her artistic observations, inspirations, and creations. "I think my blog is irreverent and tongue in cheek, just like I am," she shares. "But I hope it is also beautiful and sophisticated. I want to be proud of what people are taking their limited time to look at with my name on it."

Karen is happy with the name she has chosen to represent her and her art. "A'Musements seemed to hit all aspects of what I was after in a name—something that would lend an air of whimsy, evoke curiosity, and speak to the possibility of muses out there to help us with our creative endeavors," she says.

Because her blog is a creative one, Karen has chosen to limit her posts to those of a creative nature. "I didn't post my opinions during the presidential election, for instance, because I want my blog, which is not political but creative in nature, to stay true to that," says Karen. "I think it's sort of 'bait and switch' to lure someone in to have a quiet, enjoyable romp through a few pictures of your latest work only to have them blindsided by a political rant or religious preference."

Having a blog has enhanced Karen's life both personally and professionally. "The friendships that you make are worth their weight in gold," she says. "For my business, it has meant the difference between night and day. The blog allows people to browse my work, and be a fan before they even make a purchase. That's the best a business can hope for; a loyal and truly admiring customer. The blog makes that possible."

When asked to list a few of her favorite blogs, Karen responds, "I have 100 blogs listed on my Sites to Inspire that are all fabulous or they wouldn't be there. I try to look at these blogs each day, or every few days."

HEATHER BAILEY: Hello My Name Is Heather

Find her: heatherbailey.typepad.com
Blogs about: business, design, family, favorite things, friends, home

Heather Bailey discovered the world of blogs in September 2005, while trying to fix her broken sewing machine. Heather recalls, "A Google search brought me to a craft blog that had nothing to do with sewing machines, but everything to do with sewing, family, friendship, and discovery. Following a trail of links, I found kinship within a community of women. With their masterful paintings and quilts as well as their silly, crocheted what-nots and bizarre pincushions, these women celebrated the very thing I have centered much of my life around—creativity."

Heather immediately began researching how to start a blog and join the discussion. Hello My Name Is Heather was up and running on May 22, 2006. "Like a gaggle of strangers at a party, wearing nametags, we are all introduced by the name of our blog. I like to think my blog's name says, 'It's nice to meet you. Let's be friends,'" Heather says. "My aim is to share my love of creativity, family, friendship, and fun in my own pursuit of a happy and beautiful life, perhaps inspiring others to find joy in nurturing their families and in exploring their own creativity."

One of Heather's biggest challenges is finding the time to post. She says, "I would love to write a new post every day and to format a new free pattern or tutorial every week. But with the demands of my business and family, this pace is unrealistic. As it is, I'm pleased when I fit in three posts in a given week." Another challenge has been the technological side of blogging. "Over the years, I've enjoyed the process of developing my blog further, learning more about HTML, tables, animated gifs, etc.," says Heather. "When I first began, I didn't even know how to download images off my camera. Though I'm no expert at coding, I now have the confidence to figure things out through research and experimentation."

Heather most enjoys the love, support, and community that reaches across borders, languages, and oceans. "What a strength it is to feel the love of a worldwide community that offers helpful input, shares inspiring stories, and provides needed resources to benefit one another," she says. "It's quite an amazing thing."

Heather's favorite daily reads: blog.makezine.com, rosylittlethings.typepad.com, soulemama.typepad.com

HELLO *Heather*
my name is

Find her: allsorts.typepad.com

Blogs about: creativity, design, family, life, relationships

Jenny Harris is a children's book illustrator, designer of crafts and patterns, and maker of "all sorts" of fun items. She has been blogging since 2004 and in that time, Jenny has carved out an inspiring, creative, bright, and cheerful spot on the Web.

She started the blog after reading Loobylu.com where she got the itch to participate in Illustration Friday, a weekly creative outlet/participatory art exhibit for illustrators and artists of all skill levels. It was designed by artists Penelope Dullaghan and Brianna Privett to challenge participants creatively.

Jenny enjoyed the creative experience so much she decided to take the plunge into blogging. She sees All Sorts as "a happy place and showcase for creativity."

Jenny loves blogging because she can make it into whatever she wants it to be—no assignments, deadlines, rules, or requirements, no boss but herself. All Sorts has taught Jenny that she is much better at doing things than she thought and has empowered her with confidence. "I feel validated as a creative person, and more connected to the worldwide community of creative people," says Jenny. "I'm having a blast!"

To keep her blog interesting and a fun place to visit, Jenny regularly includes patterns, freebies, and tutorials in her posts. When asked about what inspires her, Jenny says, "Something creative gets me excited. It can be a new idea, or anything visually beautiful or different, or just silly. I like to celebrate great ideas and share the fun on my blog."

Her advice for bloggers is to blog their way. Jenny says, "Don't feel like you have to make your blog look like anyone else's. Let it be an extension of your own vision. Always be looking and learning, and most of all, have fun."

Jenny's favorite daily reads: rosylittlethings. typepad.com, angrychicken.typepad.com, weewonder fuls.com, turkeyfeathers.typepad.com, chezlarsson. typepad.com

AMY KAROL: Angry Chicken

Find her: angrychicken.typepad.com

Blogs about: cooking, creating, family, sewing

Amy Karol's blog, Angry Chicken, has become one of the most popular creative blogs on the Web. Amy says that she likes chickens and is not angry, but realizes that to everyone else she *is* the Angry Chicken…and she's cool with it. "I wish I had some funny, interesting story for how I chose the name of my blog, but I don't," says Amy. "Angry Chicken is simply part of the title of one of my favorite small quilts."

Her blog is so popular that Amy even has nicknames in blogdom, where she is referred to as "AC" or just "Chicken." Amy wouldn't change the name of her blog, but admits if she were just starting a blog now, she wouldn't give it the same name. However, she says, "It's so random and nonsensical, it suits me just fine." Amy created her blog in February 2005 as a way to

have an online sketchbook, journal, and creative outlet. She has no rules about content and describes her blog as "whatever I am into." This little chicken has been into a lot lately, from sewing to painting, knitting, and writing. Her first book, "Bend the Rules Sewing," landed on store shelves in June 2007 and a second book is in the works.

Amy's advice to bloggers is to blog from the heart and only if you want to, not if you feel you should. "Blogging shouldn't be a chore and it isn't for everyone. It's a creative medium that suits some more than others," says Amy. "If the shoe doesn't fit, try another type of creative outlet."

Amy's favorite daily reads: soulemama.typepad.com, rosylittlethings.typepad.com, theblackapple.typepad.com

angry chicken

CARRIE SOMMER: Sommer Designs Behind the Screen

Find her: sommerdesigns.typepad.com
Blogs about: business, creativity, family, inspirations

For Carrie Sommer, a designer from Southern California, her blog, Sommer Designs Behind the Screen, was going to be strictly business. She thought she would be using it to promote new products and events. However, something interesting happened: The few times she blogged about something in her personal life, her blog traffic increased. Carrie realized that her readers wanted to read more about her, her lifestyle, her inspirations, and her creative process. "This was eye opening and wonderful because it opened up so many other avenues for blogging," Carrie says.

Carrie now mixes a little bit of everything on her blog—she talks business, getting ready for events, the challenges of working at home alone, staying motivated, sourcing suppliers, and going to textile and gift shows. She combines it all with little bits of what she finds inspiring, whether it's a day spent thrift shopping or knitting, networking with other women, traveling, or cooking. No topic is off limits for this creative spirit.

"My biggest challenge is staying fresh and true to my own voice," Carrie says. Once she started to get a readership base, she began to feel an obligation to provide content. "This is the wrong reason to blog," Carrie says. She finds that blissful bloggers, herself included, are learning to blog without obligation and leave the guilt behind.

Blogging has enabled Carrie to reach across the psychological barrier of the Internet and let her customer base know that there is a person behind the computer screen, that she has a life, a family, and many dreams, inspirations, and ambitions. Her blog is aptly named Sommer Designs Behind the Screen for this reason.

Carrie says, "I am much more outgoing on my blog than in real life, and my blog has exceeded all the expectations I had."

Carrie's favorite daily reads: rosylittlethings.typepad.com, thepioneerwoman.com/confessions, decor8.blog.com

S mmer Designs...*behind the screen.*

SANDRA EVERTSON: Artful Visions and Inspirations

Find her: sandraevertson.blogspot.com
Blogs about: art, design, family, inspiration, pets

Sandra Evertson, an artist and editorial contributor to various magazines, describes her blog as "controlled lunacy." She dabbles in everything she can get her hands on, from porcelain and paper, to clay, copper, wood, and fabric. Sandra's passion for her art and life leap from the screen when you visit her blog.

When it comes to blogging, Sandra considers herself lucky to be living in a time where this sort of artistic exchange is even possible. "Blogging is so personal," she says. "Reading a blog is like stepping right into a stranger's living room, meeting their families, and seeing their artwork up close and personal. The whole spectrum of life is played out before our eyes, and we are invited to join in and come along for the virtual ride, hand in hand." It's the beautiful images that illustrate every post that allows this to happen. Though her blog's design may be simple, her posts are stunning.

Her blog entries are inspired by anything and everything. It could be something just blowing by that sets her wheels in motion. Life is always exciting and always an adventure for this talented woman.

Sandra's readers respond most to her short stories, which consist of her creating an art piece, taking photos of it, and making up a story to narrate it. The stories are whimsical, with a bit of factual history, and a good dose of humor. Sandra says her blog is, "Dr. Seuss meets a history book with a dash of DIY for good measure."

Sandra's advice for bloggers is to dive right in, be adventurous, be fearless, be expressive, be honest, and be caring and compassionate. Most of all, though, have fun. "Treat it like candy and indulge yourself in the frivolous things," she says.

Sandra's favorite daily reads: bibliodyssey.blog spot.com, cuteoverload.com, dailycoyote.net

SANDRA EVERTSON
ARTFUL VISIONS AND INSPIRATIONS

Lucky Two Shoes

Find her: decor8blog.com
Blogs about: design, fabrics, home décor

Launched in January 2006, Decor8 is a design blog dedicated to sharing decorating ideas, interiors, independent art and design, products, and services with readers in the hopes of inspiring them to live a more fulfilling and creative life.

Founder Holly Becker is a writer and interior design consultant who splits her time between New Hampshire and Germany. Maintaining residence in both countries allows her to stay on top of the latest finds and to discover a broader range of talent that may not exist yet on the Web. When Holly is in Europe, it's common for her posts to highlight her adventures at design shows, shops, and artist's studios.

Because she posts daily, Holly sets aside at least 5 to 10 hours a day for writing and researching. When she first began, her intention was to create a blog that would continuously inspire others to be more creative, to shop independent over mass-produced, and to encourage others to believe in themselves.

Holly finds gratification in knowing that the moment she publishes a post, she has the opportunity to touch someone through something she has shown or said. "It makes me happy to know that others find support and information at Decor8," says Holly. "I also hope that their souls are warmed just a little."

Holly's advice to new bloggers: "Be authentic, don't write about what you lack genuine passion for or it will show, and be supportive of other bloggers." She also suggests that you learn as much as you can about blogging etiquette.

Holly's favorite daily reads: absolutelybeautifulthings.blogspot.com, ohjoy.blogs.com, yvestown.com

weekly: *blog* That Unreliable Girl   *book* Easy Elegance

decor8
fresh finds for hip spaces

"As a writer and interior design consultant, I created decor8 to catalog beautiful finds and to inspire others." -Holly Becker

About   *Press*   *Blogroll*   *Shops*   *Faves*   *Wanted*

A Lovely Organized Closet

8

Find her: knitandtonic.typepad.com
Blogs about: knitting, life

Wendy Bernard refers to herself as the accidental blogger. After years of working in the corporate world, she became a stay-at-home mom and was looking for something to fill her time. "I never planned on my blog becoming what it is, or having a career in knitting, for that matter," she explains. "In the beginning, the only purpose was for it to be a way to practice writing and to keep busy."

When asked about her blog's unusual name, Wendy says, "It just sort of popped into my head. I guess I kinda like gin and tonics." That same open, friendly style of conversation makes readers feel right at home.

Wendy finds inspiration for her posts in simple, ordinary things. "Anything from something funny that occurred to me, or parts of the lists and notes I'm always writing to myself, to something sad that has happened," says Wendy. "It's odd that the knitting part acts as a sidekick to whatever else I write about."

She finds that her readers respond well to her more lighthearted posts. "I get the most comments in response to the funny stuff or a wacky photo or the knitting mistakes I've made," says Wendy. "Writing about things that are really personal or negative or political can bring on a lot of negative commenters. Whenever I find myself in a territory that could hurt people's feelings or in a complaining mode, I go ahead and write the post, save it, but then go back and re-read it before I decide whether I want to publish it. Once it is out there, you can't take it back."

Wendy credits her blog for many of the opportunities she has received. "The blog started my business," she says. "I didn't plan on becoming a knitwear designer or an author for that matter. Turns out, a literary agent liked reading my blog and she asked me if I wanted to write a book. When that all happened, I had designed only a few patterns for the blog and it never occurred to me that 'Custom Knits' would happen or that the next book would happen. It was all kismet, really."

Wendy's experience with blogging has been undeniably positive. She explains, "I am in awe of what happened and how lucky I am to find something that I like doing that brings me a small amount of income."

She reads other blogs when she can, but with a business and little spare time, she says she doesn't blog surf nearly enough. "I check in on friends, but I don't really have any bookmarked," says Wendy.

Original   Email Me at

DONNA O'BRIEN: The Ribboned Crown

Find her: donnaobrien.typepad.com

Blogs about: artwork, family, friends, garden, home, life

Before starting her blog, Donna O'Brien had a website by the same name where she sold her artwork. She had someone design the site and felt frustrated that she was not able to change things around herself. About that same time, Donna discovered the world of creative blogging and knew she had to join the scene. When it came time to choose a blog host, she opted for Type-Pad. "The lovely blogs I saw were on TypePad so that's the venue I chose," she says. "I had someone help me set up the basics and I learned how to read the basic codes." Nowadays, Donna manages her blog with ease.

Creating a theme on her blog was important to Donna because she loves the idea of continuity. She explains, "Because most of my artwork has a heraldic or royal feel to it I went in that direction. Categories have titles like 'pageant,' 'court,' and 'royal.'" Donna says her new digital camera has made the biggest difference on her blog. "I look back at the old photos and wish I had changed my camera sooner," she says.

The formal-sounding name of her blog gives way to a surprisingly fun and humorous place to visit. Donna's incredible images of her artwork, home, and garden are truly inspiring. Every post takes her readers on a journey and makes their day a bit brighter. "I'm a bit of a 'wise-guy' in my everyday life, and it was a challenge to let go and let that show," she says. "I kept thinking, 'How would it translate online?' Other bloggers responded positively so I knew that honesty and sincerity was the best expression for me."

For anyone thinking about starting a blog, Donna says, "Decide how much time you want and can dedicate to your blog, as it can be very time-consuming." When it comes to blogging, Donna says, "Time management is what it's cracked up to be."

Donna's favorite daily reads: awhimsicalbohemian.typepad.com, missmaddies.blogspot.com, rochambeau.typepad.com, sandraevertson.blogspot.com, ullam.typepad.com

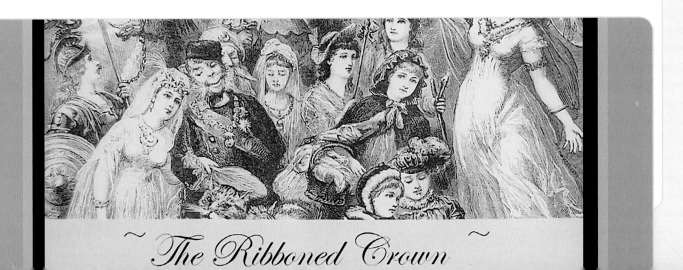

~ *The Ribboned Crown* ~

About the Author

The youngest of three children, Tara Frey was born and raised in beautiful historic Bucks County, Pennsylvania, where she still lives just a short drive from her parents and siblings. She is happily married to her high school sweetheart, Larry, and together they have two children, Nick and Natalie.

Tara is a contributing editor to several national home decorating magazines where she frequently writes about beautiful blogs and their creators, her favorite shopping sources, and decorating on a shoestring budget. She was named a "Top Romantic" in Romantic Homes magazine and has also been featured in Romantic Country magazine.

Tara blathers on about her daily life on her blog, Tara Frey {typing out loud} (tarafrey.com), where she writes about flea markets, knitting, coffeepot disasters, the Jersey shore, vintage Limoges, photography, celebrity encounters, bad haircuts, the color gray, books, magazines, corners of her home that she has dubbed "Farmhouse Chic," secret doors, giant sunglasses, an Oreo addiction, furry house guests, cozy quilts, toothless smiles, seashells, little gems, her noisy family, and her close-knit circle of friends.

Acknowledgments

Thank you to my wonderful and supportive family. To my dad, Jim, the most incredible person I know. You have been tracing your footsteps in life the old-fashioned way, putting pen to paper, creating journal after journal, that I will cherish and read forever. You are an inspiration, a teacher, and a mentor.

Thank you to my mom and biggest blog fan, Beverly. You always make me smile. I love you both more than words (or blog posts) could ever say.

Thank you to my sister, Kelly Ann, who never lets my feet get too far off the ground. I love your insane sense of humor and the laughter you bring me daily. You are always there to witness nonsensicality in the foggy mist of magical bedazzlement and glittery sparkles.

Thank you to my brother, Jimmy. I'm always proud of you. To my nieces and nephews, Jimmy Michael, Jesse, Josh, Brooke, Alex, Morgan, and Sofia, who are always interested in what I am doing and thinking Aunt T might be pretty cool after all.

Thank you to my best friends since childhood, Kristi, Rachel, and Gina (who happen to be my own personal versions of Samantha, Miranda, and Charlotte—and yes! I'm now officially Carrie). Thank you for filling my life

with so many wonderful memories along with massive amounts of giggles and allowing me to share it all with the world, bit by bit, in blog posts.

Because it took a village to make this book, thank you to the blogging community. For accepting me into your lives and being a part of mine. For encouraging me along this journey and reaching out beyond the computer screen and hugging me, every day. I am eternally grateful that you stop by my blog because I know you are busy crafting and creating, while at the same time being mothers and wives. This book is for you, and about you. Thank you to all the bloggers who contributed and helped to pull this book together, especially Chris Glynn, Sara Duckett, Heather Bullard, Catherine Haughland, and Barbara Jacksier, all of whom put up with endless emails with the word "HELP!" in the subject line and contributed far beyond the call of duty.

Thank you to Michelle Shefveland for providing the tutorial about adding frames to images. Michelle is the author of *Scrapbooking the Digital Way* (Corel/Jasc, 2003) and the owner of CottageArts.net, a digital scrapbooking resource company.

Thank you to the wonderful team at Red Lips 4 Courage. Eileen Paulin, Erika Kotite, Cathy Risling, and most of all

to Rebecca Ittner, the supreme queen of "editorness" for always being there when I needed her. To Jocelyn Foye for her incredible design and vision. Thank you, Red Lips, for believing in this book, believing in me, encouraging me along the way, and reminding me to breathe. My lips are forever red with courage.

Thank you to my ever-so-patient and kissable kids, Nicholas and Natalie, my inspiration and heartstrings, for allowing me to brag about you endlessly in blogland and being perfect in every photo. Nicholas, I adore your sweet and kind personality, and Natalie, I love your spunk and charm.

And lastly, thank you to my superhero husband. My everything. I couldn't have done this without you and your incredible support. Thank you for always believing in me. The Congressional Medal of Honor is on its way. Love you, rock star. Now, what's for dinner?

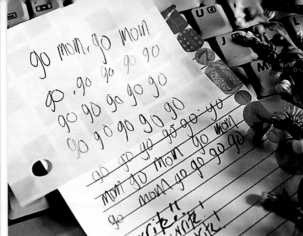

Glossary

A-List: The top bloggers who influence the blogosphere.

Archives: A collection of all previous posts on one page. Can be categorized by month, topic, etc.

Blinkies: Small, animated graphics that blink. Usually located on a blog sidebar.

Blog: Short for Web log; a website that is an online journal with interactive features.

Blog hopping: Jumping from one blog to another.

Blog tipping: When a blog author compliments three blogs on the first day of every month.

Blog vert: Also called a blogvertisment. Advertisements on a blog.

Blogebrity: A famous blogger.

Blogger: A free blogging platform offered by Google (uniqueblogname.blogspot.com); someone who blogs.

Blogging: The act of writing an online journal/web log.

Blogiday: A vacation from blogging.

Blogiversary: The birthdate of a blog.

Blogoholic: Someone who's addicted to blogging.

Blogosphere: The global community of web blogs.

Blogroll: A list of favorite links on a sidebar.

Blogsit: Maintaining/writing a blog while the primary blogger is on leave.

Blogsite: A website that combines blog feeds from numerous sources.

Blogsnob: A blogger who refuses to respond to blog comments left by those outside of their "clique."

Blogspeak: A language developed for and used in Internet journals, or blogs, by their authors, who are also known as bloggers.

Blogstar: A blogger running a popular blog.

Blogvertising: Also called a blog vert. Advertising on a blog.

Browser: A Web browser; a software application that enables a user to display and interact with text, images, videos, music, games, and other information typically located on a web page.

CAPTCHA: Acronym for Completely Automated Public Turing Test to Tell Computers and Humans Apart. Used to tell computers and humans apart. These are the word and letter verification images you type in to be allowed to leave comments. The most common type of CAPTCHA found on blogs requires that the user type the letters of a distorted sequence of letters or numbers that appears on the screen.

Categories: Links on a blog sidebar that contain similar types of posts. Categories help readers find posts written on general topics. Categories can include family, crafting, sewing, jewelry, shows, and tips.

Chronological order: Blog posts automatically added at the top of the blog's home page. As new posts are added to the top of the page, older posts move down the page.

CMS: Acronym for Content Management System. A type of software used to publish and manage blogs and websites.

Comment: A response written by a reader to a blog post. Comments are the interactive feature that makes blogs different than a static web page.

Comment spam: Like email spam, comment spam is an unsolicited, unwanted comment that has nothing to do with the post it is connected to.

Commenter: Someone who leaves a written comment on a blog.

Content: Basically, the material on a blog or website, including documents, posts, images, audio and video files, and more.

Copyright: A legal concept or term that gives the creator of an original work of authorship or art exclusive rights to control the distribution of that work for a certain period of time. In general terms, it is "a right to copy," but it usually gives the individual other rights like the right to be credited for the work, to determine who can adapt or perform the work, etc. The modern intent of copyright is to promote the creation of new works by providing authors control of, and profit from, their work.

CSS: Acronym for Cascading Style Sheets. A language used to write a set of rules about the layout and appearance of a website.

Dashboard: The first screen you see when logging into your blogging account. It shows all of the controls, functions, and tools.

Developer-hosted software: The most popular type of software used by creative bloggers, developer-hosted platforms do the work, and you don't need to know any tech jargon to get started. Once your blog is set up, posting and adding images and sidebar information is pretty simple. Some companies charge fees, while others are free.

Digital SLR: A digital single-lens reflex camera (also known as a DSLR) that uses a mechanical mirror system and a five-sided prism (known as a pentaprism) to direct light from the camera lens to an optical viewfinder on the back of the camera.

Domain: Also known as domain name or host name. It is the name that identifies a website on the Internet. For example, yahoo.com is a domain name, but www.yahoo.com is not a domain, it is a URL.

Domain mapping: The process of pointing a registered domain name to a website, blog, or an online photo album.

Doppelblogger: Someone who plagiarizes the content of another blogger.

Download: To receive data from a remote or central system, such as a web server, FTP server, or mail server; any file offered for downloading or that has been downloaded.

Filtering software: Also known as a filter. 1.) A computer program to process a data stream. It accepts a certain type of data as input, transforms it in some manner, and then outputs the transformed data. 2.) Sometimes utilities that allow a user to import or export data are also called filters. 3.) A set pattern through which data is passed. Only data that matches the pattern is allowed to pass through the filter.

Flickr: A free online photo management and sharing application. Enables users to upload photos to their site, create photo albums, and share videos and images with others.

FTP: Acronym for File Transfer Protocol. A standard Internet protocol, it is the simplest way to exchange files between computers on the Internet. FTP is often used to transfer web page files from their creator's computer to the computer that acts as its server for everyone on the Internet. It is also used to download files and programs to your computer from other servers.

Graphic ad: An ad that appears on a website or blog sidebar that is made using a banner image. These ads always link to the website that is buying the ad space.

Host blogger: The owner of a blog who writes and publishes posts on that blog.

Hosting service: A software platform used to host a blog. Types include user-hosted platforms, free multi-user platforms, and developer-hosted software.

HTML: Acronym for HyperText Markup Language. A language used to mark the elements of a document to create a web page.

Icerocket: A free software product, Icerocket (icerocket. com) is a blog search engine. It is also an invisible tracker that counts visits to your blog and other blog statistics.

IP address: Acronym for Internet Protocol Address. A logical address (or numerical identification) assigned to devices in a computer network that use the Internet Protocol for communication between its nodes.

Linkback: A method for blog authors to obtain notifications when other authors link to one of their documents. This enables authors to keep track of who is linking to, or referring to, their articles. The three methods of link-backs—Refback, Trackback, and Pingback—differ in how they accomplish this task.

Load time: The time that a website takes to load, usually a matter of seconds. The faster the load time, the better. Research suggests that a majority of users will skip a blog or website if it fails to load within five seconds.

Lurker: A blog reader who does not post comments, they just take an occasional look.

Multi-user platforms: Software packages used by blog authors and domain owners to run on their own systems. They can be free or paid.

Niche blog: A blog that focuses on a specific topic or subject. Examples include news, art, education, crafts, sports, gossip, humor, and finance.

Photo sharing: The publishing or transfer of a user's digital photos online. This allows the user to share them with others (publicly or privately).

Photobucket: A free online photo management application (photobucket.com) that lets users upload, share, link to, and find images, videos, and graphics.

Pingback: One of three types of linkbacks. A method for blog authors to request notification when somebody links to one of their documents. WordPress supports automatic pingbacks (where all the links can be pinged when the article is published). Because of the way pingbacks work, they are less prone to spam than trackbacks (another type of linkback).

Plug-in: A small file that adds improved functionality and new features to your blog.

Podcast: A series of audio or video digital-media files distributed over the Internet through Web feeds and to portable media players and personal computers.

Post: An entry written and published on a blog; to write an entry on a blog.

Problogger: A professional blogger.

Profile: Information contained on a blog about the blog owner. Usually accessed by a clickable link found on the blog home page. Includes the blogger's name, contact information, hobbies, career, passions, and likes/dislikes.

Reciprocal links: Links posted on one person's blog to another blogger.

Refback: One of three types of linkbacks; a method for bloggers to request notification when somebody links to one of their documents. This enables authors to keep track of who is linking to, or referring to, their articles.

RSS feed: RSS (Real Simple Syndication, also known as Rich Site Summary) is a format for delivering regularly updated Web content such as blogs. Visitors to your blog can click on the RSS feed link and they will automatically be notified when your blog is updated.

Search engine: A search engine is designed to search for information on the World Wide Web. Popular search engines include: Google, Live Search, Yahoo! Search, AOL Search, Ask.com, Lycos, and AltaVista. Results of a

search may consist of Web pages, images, information, and other types of files.

SEO: Acronym for Search Engine Optimization. Includes several activities geared toward improving the rankings of a blog inside the results page of search engines. Optimizing a blog with SEO includes editing and writing content and HTML code with the purpose of increasing relevance to specific keywords to search engines.

Sidebar: One or more columns along one or both sides of a blog's main page.

Tag awards: Recognition by a blogger who "tags" another blogger for having an "award-winning" blog.

Tags: A simple category name. Bloggers can categorize their posts and images with anything they think makes sense. See Category.

Technorati: A real-time search engine for blogs that keeps track of what is going on in the blogosphere. Its most famous feature is the Technorati Top 100 list, which ranks the largest (and most visited) blogs in the world. Find them at technorati.com.

Template: Blog presentation design.

Trackback: One of three types of linkbacks; a method for blog authors to request notification when somebody links to one of their documents. This enables bloggers to keep track of who is linking to their articles.

TypePad: A domain-hosted paid blogging software platform created and owned by Six Apart Ltd.

URL: Acronym for Uniform Resource Locator; a compact string of characters used to identify a resource on the Internet. A URL includes a domain name and a protocol to be used. For example, when a browser sees the URL https://www.domain.com it knows that it needs to send a secure http request to the host domain.

User-hosted platforms: Software packages installed by blog authors to run on their own servers.

Web feed: Allows online users to subscribe to websites that change or add content regularly. See RSS.

Web host: A type of Internet hosting service that allows individuals and organizations to make their own website accessible via the World Wide Web. Web hosts are companies that provide space on a server they own as well as provide Internet connectivity.

Webring: A collection of similar websites from around the Internet joined together. Each site in the webring contains links to the previous site and next site.

Widget: Software tools and content (such as a button, entry field, or drop-down list) you can add, arrange, and remove from the sidebar area of your blog.

Wiki: A collaborative online software program that allows readers to create and edit web page content. Wikis are useful for collaboration, collection of information, research, and class projects. Wikipedia is the most well-known example.

WordPress: A free domain-hosted blog software platform.

Index

Resources

Online resources abound to help you do everything blog related. The following list will help you create your own blissful blog.

Design & Templates: barijonline.com, becomeablogger.com, bighugelabs. com/flickr, bloggingthemes.com, dailyblogtips.com, etsy.com (keyword: blog banner design), lenatoewsdesigns. blogspot.com, sadieolive.com, theaval onrose.com

Backgrounds & Wallpapers: eblogtem plates.com, onecuteblog.blogspot.com, smittenblogdesignsgallery.blogspot. com, theavalonrose.com, thecutestblog ontheblock.com

Platforms: blogger.com, hubpages. com, livejournal.com, movabletype.com, tumblr.com, typepad.com, vox.com, wordpress.com, xanga.com

Digital Photography Help & Tutorials: cottagearts.net, digicamhelp.com, digi tal1to1.com, digital-photography-school. com, gettotallyrad.com, bighugelabs. com/flickr, theavalonrose.com/tutorials

Domain Names & Hosting: domain.com, godaddy.com, networksolutions.com

Fonts: dafonts.com, misprintedtype.com, myfonts.com, urbanfonts.com, veer.com

Photo-Editing Software: adobe.com/ photoshop, corel.com, picasa.google. com, serif.com/photoplus, ulead.com/pi

Photo & Video Hosting: flickr.com, pho tobucket.com, slide.com, youtube.com

Subscriber Feeds: rss.com

Thank you to The Farm Chicks for the use of their flower graphic on the book spine and to Lisa Tutman Oglesby for the use of her banner on the back cover

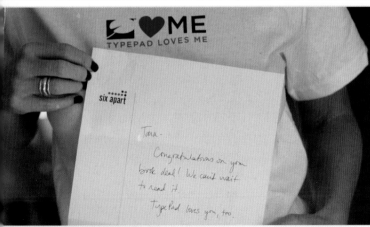